DINOSAURS
of the World

with an Introduction by
Mark Norell

American Museum of Natural History
Co curator, Halls of Dinosaurs and Hall of Vertebrate Origins

Consultants
Michael Benton

Professor of Vertebrate Paleontology, University of Bristol
Codirector, The Dinosaur Society

Tom Holtz

Assistant Research Scientist and Lecturer in Vertebrate Paleontology,
Department of Geology, University of Maryland

Edited by
Chris Marshall

6

Kritosaurus – Nodosaurus

Marshall Cavendish
New York . London . Toronto . Sydney

Marshall Cavendish Corporation
99 White Plains Road
Tarrytown, New York 10591-9001

Printed and bound in Italy

Library of Congress Cataloging-in-Publication Data

Dinosaurs of the world / with an introduction by Mark Norell ;
  consultants, Michael Benton, Tom Holtz ; edited by Chris Marshall.
      p. cm.
    Includes bibliographical references and index.
    Contents: 1. Abelisaurus–Arrhinoceratops — 2. Avialans
–Chasmosaurus — 3. Chialingosaurus–Diplodocus — 4. Dromaeosaurs
–Geological time — 5. Giganotosaurus–Kentrosaurus — 6. Kritosaurus
–Nodosaurus — 7. Omeisaurus–Plants — 8. Plateosaurus–Sauropelta —
9. Sauropodomorph dinosaurs–Syntarsus — 10. Talarurus
–Zephyrosaurus — 11. Index.
    ISBN 0-7614-7072-7 (set : lib. bdg. : acid-free paper)
    1. Dinosaurs—Encyclopedias, Juvenile. 2. Paleontology—
  Encyclopedias, Juvenile. [1. Dinosaurs—Encyclopedias.
  2. Paleontology—Encyclopedias.]   I. Marshall, Chris. II. Marshall
  Cavendish Corporation.
  OE862.D5D524   1998
  567.9'03—DC21   97–43365
                                                                CIP
                                                                AC

    ISBN 0-7614-7072-7 (set)
    ISBN 0-7614-7078-6 (vol. 6)

Picture credits
Color illustrations: Arril Johnson 360, 368–369, 382–383; Steve Kirk 330, 332–333, 344–345, 366–367, 374, 378–379; James G. Robins 334–335, 338–339, 350–351, 354–355, 362–363, 376–377; Steve White 328, 342, 346, 348–349, 358, 372, 380–381. The publishers would also like to thank Salamander Picture Library for permission to use the following color illustration by John Sibbick: 326.
Photographs: David Middleton/NHPA 335 (t), Adrian Warren/Ardea, London 340 (b); Y. Arthus-Bertrand/Ardea, London 356 (t); Museum of Natural History, Oxford University 363 (t), 364; Tom Brakefield/Corbis 370.

BROWN PARTWORKS

Editor: Chris Marshall
Assistant editors: Shona Grimbly, Alex MacKenzie, Matthew Turner, Clint Twist
Art editors: Steve Wilson, Graham Curd
Picture researcher: Brigitte Arora
Color illustrations: Arril Johnson, Steve Kirk, James G. Robins, Steve White (all of The Dinosaur Society Artists' Guild)
Line art and silhouettes: Guy Smith, Mainline Design; Denise Blagden and David Nicholls©Salamander Picture Library
Maps and family trees:
Colin Woodman
Authors: Paul Barrett (University of Cambridge), Donald Henderson (University of Bristol), Tom Holtz (University of Maryland), James I. Kirkland (Dinamation International Society), Mark Norell (American Museum of Natural History). With additional material by Liz Cook, David Gower, Jo Wright (all of the University of Bristol).

MARSHALL CAVENDISH CORPORATION

Editorial director: Paul Bernabeo
Project editor: Debra M. Jacobs

The Consultants
Michael Benton is Professor of Vertebrate Paleontology at the University of Bristol. He has a Ph. D. from the University of Newcastle and has had a research career of over 20 years. He works on the origin of the dinosaurs and other animals of the Triassic period. He has published 30 books, from popular works about dinosaurs and prehistoric life to basic textbooks on paleontology.

Tom Holtz is an Assistant Research Scientist and Lecturer at the University of Maryland, College Park. He has a Ph. D. from Yale University and specializes in theropod evolution. He works on the origin and behavior of *Tyrannosaurus* and other tyrannosaurs. He has published many articles and technical papers on dinosaurs and has taken part in dinosaur documentaries in the US and overseas.

Contents

articles on ornithischian dinosaurs ■ articles on saurischian dinosaurs ■ articles on general topics

The tree of life

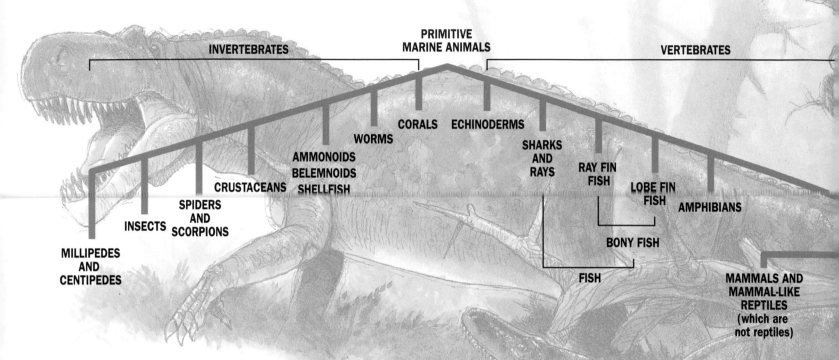

INVERTEBRATES | PRIMITIVE MARINE ANIMALS | VERTEBRATES

MILLIPEDES AND CENTIPEDES
INSECTS
SPIDERS AND SCORPIONS
CRUSTACEANS
AMMONOIDS BELEMNOIDS SHELLFISH
WORMS
CORALS
ECHINODERMS
SHARKS AND RAYS
RAY FIN FISH
LOBE FIN FISH
BONY FISH
FISH
AMPHIBIANS
MAMMALS AND MAMMAL-LIKE REPTILES (which are not reptiles)

The history of life looks a bit like an upside-down tree. A common ancestor at the top diverges into different branches, and these branches into even more branches, and so on. The branches represent different groups of life-forms.

Scientists seek to understand just how this tree grew and how life-forms are related to one another. One of their methods is to identify special features. Every living thing has its own unique mix of features, for example, types of bones or numbers of fingers. Some features will be new (they have evolved on their own), and some features will be old (they were inherited from ancestors). By studying these features, or traits, we can climb backward

on the tree of life to find out how different kinds of living things are related.

Let's start with birds. If you examined a bird's skeleton, you would find that it has a flexible neck joint. The first theropod (two-legged meat-eating dinosaur) also had a flexible neck joint. In our tree of life, a group of organisms includes the common ancestor and all of its descendants. For example, the theropod group includes the first theropod and all of its descendants, so scientists identify our bird as a theropod. The bird has a long neck that it inherited from the first saurischian dinosaur, so the bird is also considered a saurischian dinosaur. The bird's hip sockets allow it to walk

with its legs held beneath its body. It inherited these hips from the first dinosaur, so our bird is also considered to be a dinosaur. The holes in its skull in front of its eye sockets came from the first archosaur, so we group it as an archosaur. Our bird has scales around its feet, which it inherited from its reptile ancestors, so it is also part of the reptile branch of the tree of life. Our bird has a backbone inside its body, so, like mammals, amphibians, and fish, it is also a vertebrate.

This diagram shows how groups of animals are linked. By following the tree upward from birds or from any group of animals, you can find out how the different groups of animals are related.

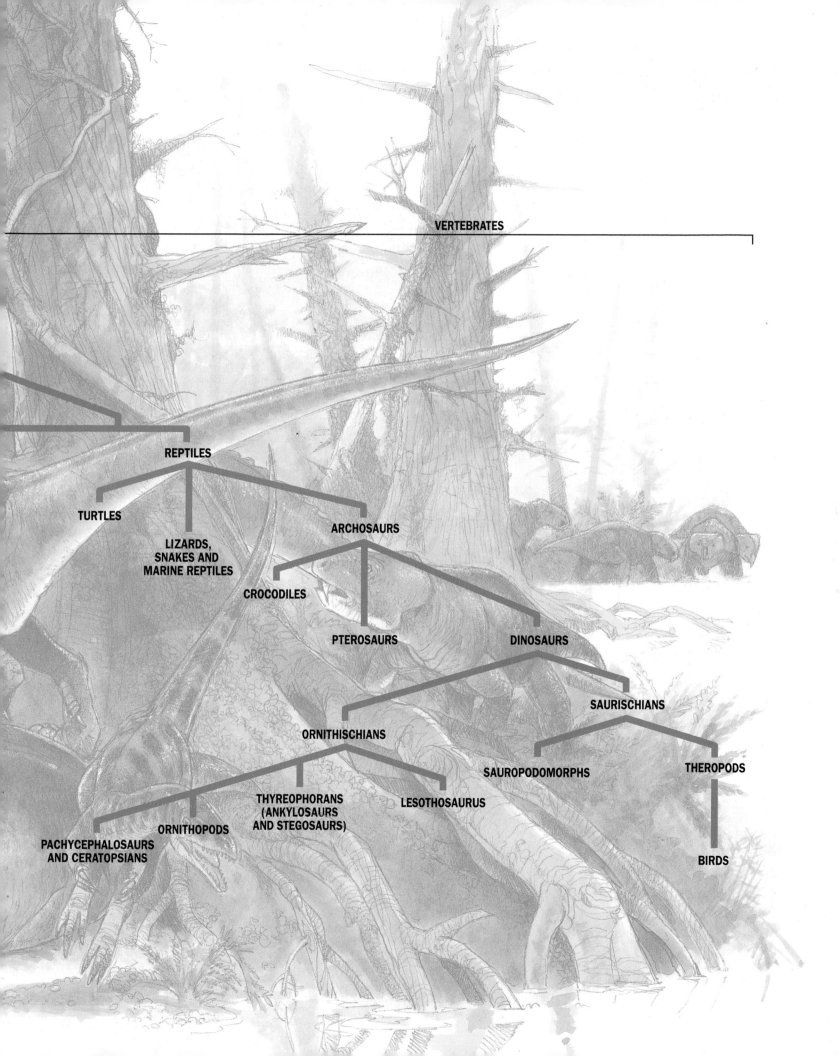

VERTEBRATES

REPTILES

TURTLES

LIZARDS,
SNAKES AND
MARINE REPTILES

ARCHOSAURS

CROCODILES

PTEROSAURS

DINOSAURS

SAURISCHIANS

ORNITHISCHIANS

SAUROPODOMORPHS

THEROPODS

PACHYCEPHALOSAURS
AND CERATOPSIANS

ORNITHOPODS

THYREOPHORANS
(ANKYLOSAURS
AND STEGOSAURS)

LESOTHOSAURUS

BIRDS

Kritosaurus

Kritosaurus was one of the hadrosaurs (duckbill dinosaurs). It lived on lush, leafy plains during the Late Cretaceous period, cropping and crunching plants with its horny beak and tough cheek teeth.

Kritosaurus was one of the biggest and heaviest hadrosaurs. US fossil-hunter Barnum Brown found the first remains of *Kritosaurus* in 1904, while collecting for the American Museum of Natural History.

Kritosaurus had a wide, flat skull. Like other hadrosaurs, it had a broad snout that looked

SKIN AND BONES

Osteoderms are hard, bony plates that are buried in the skin of many reptiles. These plates form a flexible armor that helps protect an animal from attack. Crocodiles are among the best examples of animals living today that have osteoderms. Crocodile osteoderms are shaped like triangles, squares, and diamonds. The underside of an osteoderm is usually smooth. The top is pitted and rough.

Fossilized osteoderms are rarely found in place because they were fixed into the skin layers, not to the main bones of the skeleton. If a dinosaur carcass fell in a river, the skin usually rotted first, scattering the osteoderms all over the place. The paleontologist can only guess where to put the osteoderms. Did the dinosaur have 2 rows of these bony plates or 20? Were the osteoderms along the back, up the neck, along the tail, down the sides? Luckily, when fossil-hunters found *Kritosaurus*, its osteoderms were more or less in place.

◄ *Kritosaurus* belonged to a group of hadrosaurs known as hadrosaurines. Unlike other hadrosaurs, they had no head crests or only small ones. The bump in front of its eyes is sometimes described as a "Roman nose."

like a duck's bill. On its nose was a bump. Females may not have had this bump. If so, males may have used their bumps to show off to females.

A low ridge ran along *Kritosaurus*'s neck, back, and tail. The ridge was made of tall bones that stuck out from its backbones. Stiff cords (tendons) linked the spines, turning them into a smooth ridge. When the animal was alive, the ridge was covered by a layer of skin and small, bony plates called osteoderms. Set into the skin, the osteoderms protected *Kritosaurus* from harm during an attack.

How *Kritosaurus* lived

Kritosaurus lived on plains near the sea where trees and low bushes grew. It had a toothless beak at the front of its mouth, and rows of teeth packed into the sides of its jaws.

Kritosaurus gathered tough leaves and twigs in its beak and chewed them with its cheek teeth. Many dinosaurs could not chew; they had no cheeks so the food would have fallen out of their mouths if they had tried. Ornithopods (bird-footed dinosaurs), such as *Kritosaurus* and *Hadrosaurus*, had cheeks, so they could chew. They could also move their upper jaws from side to side to grind their upper teeth across their lower teeth.

CHECK THESE OUT!

Collecting dinosaurs, Cretaceous period, Hadrosaurs, *Hadrosaurus*, Ornithischian dinosaurs, Ornithopods

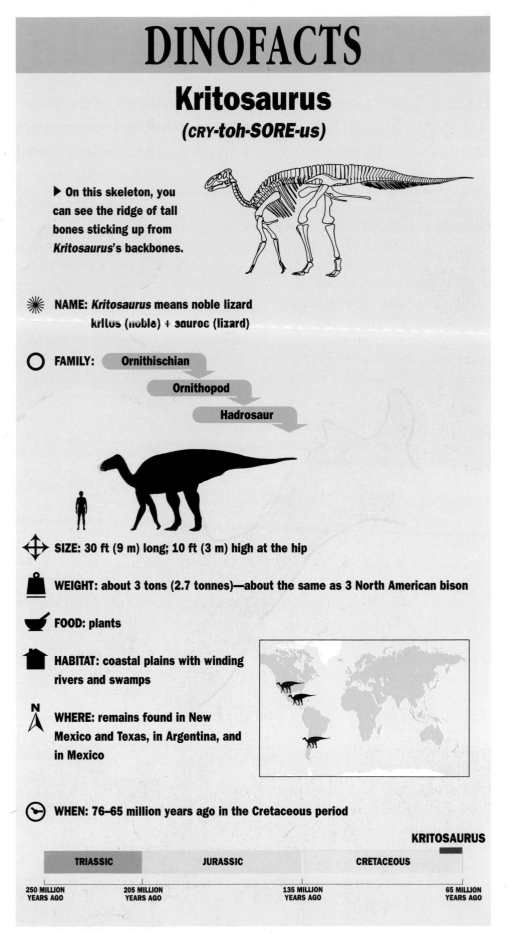

DINOFACTS

Kritosaurus
(CRY-*toh*-SORE-us)

▶ On this skeleton, you can see the ridge of tall bones sticking up from *Kritosaurus*'s backbones.

✳ **NAME:** *Kritosaurus* means noble lizard
kritos (noble) + sauros (lizard)

○ **FAMILY:** Ornithischian → Ornithopod → Hadrosaur

✢ **SIZE:** 30 ft (9 m) long; 10 ft (3 m) high at the hip

WEIGHT: about 3 tons (2.7 tonnes)—about the same as 3 North American bison

FOOD: plants

HABITAT: coastal plains with winding rivers and swamps

WHERE: remains found in New Mexico and Texas, in Argentina, and in Mexico

⏱ **WHEN:** 76–65 million years ago in the Cretaceous period

			KRITOSAURUS
TRIASSIC	JURASSIC	CRETACEOUS	
250 MILLION YEARS AGO	205 MILLION YEARS AGO	135 MILLION YEARS AGO	65 MILLION YEARS AGO

Lambeosaurus

In the Late Cretaceous period, North America was home to many kinds of hadrosaurs, or duckbill dinosaurs. One of the largest of these dinosaurs was *Lambeosaurus* or Lambe's lizard.

Lambeosaurus was named in honor of Lawrence Lambe, a Canadian scientist who hunted dinosaurs from 1897 to 1915. Among other dinosaurs, Lambe studied hadrosaurs (duckbills), and that is what *Lambeosaurus* was. Because many good specimens of different sizes, sexes, and ages have been found, *Lambeosaurus* is one of the best-known hadrosaurs. It was also one of the largest. Its strong bones helped this big animal move around.

◀ A *Lambeosaurus* with a disklike crest and another with a double spike. These could be male and female of the same kind (species) of *Lambeosaurus*.

The head crest

There were two kinds of hadrosaurs—those that had hollow head crests and those that did not. *Lambeosaurus* had a hollow crest, so all hollow-crested duckbills are called lambeosaurines. Duckbills that did not have hollow crests, like *Hadrosaurus*, are called hadrosaurines.

Lambeosaurus had some of the oddest head crests of all. Not all *Lambeosaurus* had similar crests—there were

DINOFACTS

Lambeosaurus
(LAM-bee-oh-SORE-us)

 NAME: *Lambeosaurus* means Lambe's lizard
Lambe (scientist Lawrence Lambe) + sauros (lizard)

 FAMILY:

Ornithischian
Ornithopod
Hadrosaur

SIZE: 30 ft (9 m) long; 10 ft (3 m) high at the hip

WEIGHT: about 5–10 tons (4.5–9 tonnes)—about the same as 1–2 African elephants

 FOOD: plants

HABITAT: dry lowland plains

 **WHERE:** remains found in Montana, in Alberta, Canada, and in Mexico

▶ Many *Lambeosaurus* had large, helmetlike crests. Most of the crest was hollow, but at the back was a backward-pointing spike of solid bone.

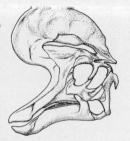

🕐 **WHEN:** 76–72 million years ago in the Cretaceous period

LAMBEOSAURUS

TRIASSIC	JURASSIC	CRETACEOUS	
250 MILLION YEARS AGO	205 MILLION YEARS AGO	135 MILLION YEARS AGO	65 MILLION YEARS AGO

TROMBONE NOSE

Much of *Lamboesaurus*'s crest was hollow. Tubes connected it to the dinosaur's nose on the inside. Paleontologists believe that *Lambeosaurus* may have used its crest like a horn. It may have been able to sound off to other *Lambeosaurus* by blowing through it. Because the bony crest could not change shape, it could produce only one type of sound.

Lambeosaurus was probably most closely related to *Corythosaurus* and *Hypacrosaurus*. These two lambeosaurine hadrosaurs also had large, hollow crests.

many different shapes and sizes. Their crests looked like disks, helmets, or double spikes.

Because of the different crests, paleontologists used to think that many kinds of *Lambeosaurus* existed. Later studies, though, suggested that the crests became bigger as *Lambeosaurus* grew older. Adult males' crests may also have been bigger than females' crests. This new information made paleontologists change their ideas. They now think there were perhaps only one or two different kinds of *Lambeosaurus*. The different

crests really belonged to males, females, and young of these same one or two kinds.

How *Lambeosaurus* lived
Like all ornithischians, *Lambeosaurus* ate plants. It lived alongside at least nine other hadrosaurs, including *Corythosaurus*.

CHECK THESE OUT!

Corythosaurus, Cretaceous period, Hadrosaurs, *Hadrosaurus*, *Hypacrosaurus*, Ornithischian dinosaurs, Ornithopods

Leaellynasaura

For a long time, most scientists thought that dinosaurs lived only in warm habitats, but new discoveries prove that dinosaurs lived in cooler places as well. One of these new finds is *Leaellynasaura*.

Fossil-hunters have found many pieces of *Leaellynasaura* remains in quarries in Australia—bits of skulls, tail bones, legs, and toes. From these few scraps, however, scientists can imagine how *Leaellynasaura* looked in life by comparing it to similar, better-known dinosaurs.

How *Leaellynasaura* lived
Leaellynasaura was an ornithischian (bird-hipped) dinosaur. Like all ornithischians

BIG BRAINS, BIG EYES

One special feature of the *Leaellynasaura* fossils is that the skulls contain natural casts, or molds, of the brain formed as the remains fossilized. Scientists can measure the volume of these brain casts, and estimate how intelligent *Leaellynasaura* was. By comparing the brain volume of *Leaellynasaura* with that of lizards, birds, and mammals that are alive today, we see that *Leaellynasaura* was probably smarter than most other dinosaurs, and certainly much smarter than any lizard or crocodile.

Leaellynasaura's brain cast shows us something else, too. The parts of the brain that are important for vision are large. *Leaellynasaura* also seems to have had very large eyes. These two facts suggest that *Leaellynasaura* could see really well. Some scientists think that *Leaellynasaura* may have been able to see well in low light during long, dark winters. If *Leaellynasaura* was adapted for seeing on dull winter days, then perhaps it did not migrate to avoid the winter cold.

▼ *Leaellynasaura* lived in Australia when that country had very cold weather. While some scientists think the dinosaur might have headed for warmer areas during the icy winters, others do not.

it ate plants. Other dinosaurs closely related to *Leaellynasaura*, such as *Hypsilophodon*, had a turtlelike beak, so *Leaellynasaura* probably had a beak, too. A beak can grow faster than teeth can. Because it is also softer than teeth, it can be worn down to just the right shape for nipping leaves off the branches of bushes.

Coping with the cold

This cool–climate dinosaur was found in Australia—a hot, dry country today. During the Cretaceous period, though, the positions of the continents were different than they are now. Australia was much farther south and was joined to Antarctica. It would have had cool, even freezing, winters. How did *Leaellynasaura* deal with the cold weather?

Some scientists think the dinosaur could stand the cold. However, other scientists point out that if it had naked skin, it would have had a hard time keeping warm. Also there would be no food in winter.

These scientists think that *Leaellynasaura* may have migrated every year. It would spend the long summer days feeding on plants close to the South Pole. When the cooler fall and winter weather arrived, *Leaellynasaura* would move closer to the warmer equator.

CHECK THESE OUT!

Continental drift, Cretaceous period, Crocodiles, *Hypsilophodon*, Lizards and snakes, Ornithischian dinosaurs, Ornithopods

Leaellynasaura

(*LEE-ah-LIN-ah-SORE-ah*)

✳ **NAME:** *Leaellynasaura* means Leaellyn's lizard
Leaellyn (the name of a girl who helped dig the fossils) + saura (lizard)

◯ **FAMILY:** Ornithischian → Ornithopod

✛ **SIZE:** 3 ft (90 cm) long; perhaps about 1 ft (30 cm) high at the hip

▉ **WEIGHT:** 10–15 lbs (4.5–7 kg)—about the same as a large chicken or small turkey

⚱ **FOOD:** low-growing plants

⌂ **HABITAT:** well-watered upland valleys

⇡ **WHERE:** remains found in Australia

🕑 **WHEN:** about 110 million years ago during the Cretaceous period

			LEAELLYNASAURA	
TRIASSIC		JURASSIC		CRETACEOUS
250 MILLION YEARS AGO	205 MILLION YEARS AGO		135 MILLION YEARS AGO	65 MILLION YEARS AGO

Leptoceratops

Leptoceratops was a ceratopsian, or horned dinosaur, but it had hardly any of the features that most horned dinosaurs had. Even today, scientists are not sure how to describe it.

US fossil-hunter Barnum Brown first described *Leptoceratops* in 1914 from a partial skeleton and skull found in Alberta, Canada. In the 1940s, Canadian paleontologist Charles M. Sternberg collected some *Leptoceratops* remains that were in better condition.

SWIMMING AGAINST THE TIDE

Scientists see patterns (trends) in the way the horned dinosaurs evolved. Early ceratopsians like *Psittacosaurus* were small, two-legged walkers with simple skulls. Over time, ceratopsians grew horns, neck frills, and much bigger bodies. By the Late Cretaceous period, *Triceratops* had evolved, a horn-faced heavy that could tough it out with big meat-eaters. However, some ceratopsians like *Leptoceratops* and *Microceratops* went against the trend. They stayed simple, small, and fast.

▼ Little *Leptoceratops* had a light body and slender limbs. Scientists are not sure whether it moved only on its hind legs, or only on all fours, or both.

Little ceratopsian

Leptoceratops was a primitive (less evolved) ceratopsian. Most advanced (highly evolved) ceratopsians were large; mighty *Triceratops* was the size of two elephants. More primitive ceratopsians, like *Protoceratops*, *Bagaceratops*, and *Psittacosaurus*, could be smaller than a pig.

Leptoceratops
(*LEP-toe-SER-ah-tops*)

✳ **NAME:** *Leptoceratops* means slender horned face
leptos (slender) + keratos (horned) + ops (face)

○ **FAMILY:** Ornithischian
Ceratopsian

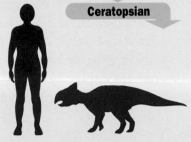

✛ **SIZE:** 6 ft (1.8 m) long; 2.5 ft (76 cm) high at the hip

⚖ **WEIGHT:** 100–150 lbs (45–68 kg)—about the same as a pronghorn

⚗ **FOOD:** tough, low-growing plants

🏠 **HABITAT:** upland plains

🧭 **WHERE:** remains found in Alberta, Canada; and Wyoming

▶ Like other ceratopsians, *Leptoceratops* had a beak. However, it had only a small neck frill.

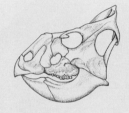

🕐 **WHEN:** 70–65 million years ago in the Cretaceous period

			LEPTOCERATOPS
TRIASSIC	JURASSIC	CRETACEOUS	
250 MILLION YEARS AGO	205 MILLION YEARS AGO	135 MILLION YEARS AGO	65 MILLION YEARS AGO

Like these, *Leptoceratops* was small. Advanced ceratopsians had horns on their faces and bony frills on the back of their heads. *Leptoceratops* had no horns, and its head frill was unusually small.

On two legs?

Most Late Cretaceous ceratopsians walked on all fours. Because most of its body weight was in front of its hips, *Leptoceratops* may have walked on all fours, too. However, because its hind legs were longer than its front limbs, some scientists believe that *Leptoceratops* walked on its hind legs only. Early Cretaceous *Psittacosaurus* also moved around on its hind legs. Because *Leptoceratops* lacked a big frill and might have walked on two legs, some scientists think it might have been as primitive as *Psittacosaurus*.

How *Leptoceratops* lived

All ceratopsians had beak bones at the front of their mouths. In life, horn covered the bone to form the beak. *Leptoceratops* had a beak, and probably had strong jaw muscles too, which gave it a powerful bite for chopping up tough plant materials.

Leptoceratops would have made a tasty meal for almost any Late Cretaceous meat-eater. It probably ran fast to flee predators or hid in thick bushes to avoid big killers such as *Tyrannosaurus*.

CHECK THESE OUT!

Bagaceratops, Ceratopsians, Cretaceous period, Evolution, Ornithischian dinosaurs, Protoceratops, Psittacosaurus, Triceratops, Tyrannosaurus

Lesothosaurus

When most people hear the word *dinosaur* they think of animals as big as city buses; however, much smaller dinosaurs also existed.

Lesothosaurus was a tiny dinosaur. In life it would not have been more than about 3.3 ft (1 m) long. Even so, *Lesothosaurus* is an important dinosaur because it was one of the earliest members of a group of dinosaurs known as the ornithischian, or bird-hipped, dinosaurs. All the ornithischian dinosaurs were plant-eaters.

The secrets of teeth

Paleontologists know that *Lesothosaurus* ate plants, because of the shape of its teeth. Its teeth were not like the long, serrated blades of the meat-eating dinosaurs, such as *Tyrannosaurus* and *Velociraptor*. *Lesothosaurus*'s front teeth were cone-shaped. The rest of its teeth were like little triangular leaves stuck on top of long, narrow bases, or roots. *Lesothosaurus*'s teeth were about 0.5–0.75 in (1–2 cm) long.

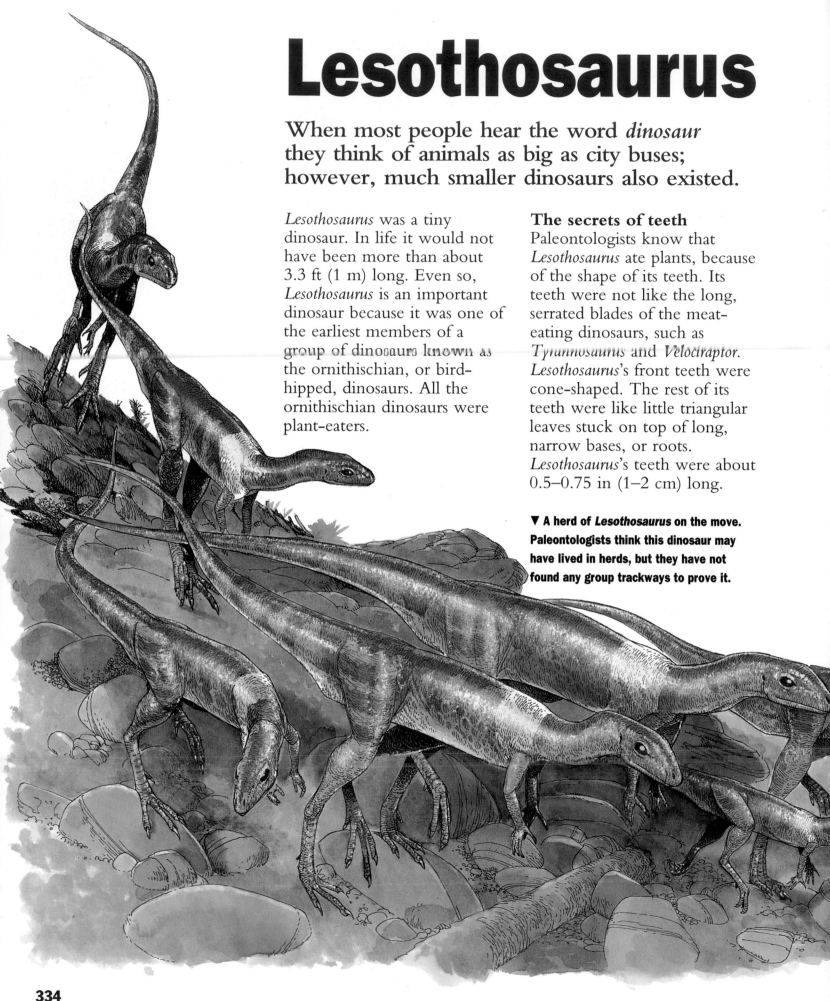

▼ A herd of *Lesothosaurus* on the move. Paleontologists think this dinosaur may have lived in herds, but they have not found any group trackways to prove it.

The longest part of a *Lesothosaurus* tooth was the root. All dinosaurs had teeth with long roots. The roots of the teeth were fixed into deep sockets along the upper and lower edges of the jaws. This made the teeth very strong, and let dinosaurs bite and chew many different foods.

Tearing teeth

The top parts of *Lesothosaurus*'s teeth, the triangular parts, had roughened edges. These rough edges helped *Lesothosaurus* to tear bushes and ferns.

As *Lesothosaurus* closed its jaws, the rough edges of its upper teeth would meet the rough edges of its lower teeth. This chopping and cutting action might have helped to tear its food into pieces small enough to swallow.

Like more advanced (highly evolved) ornithischian dinosaurs, *Lesothosaurus* had cheeks. They were not as muscular as those of advanced ornithischians, but they probably allowed *Lesothosaurus*

▲ Like this tortoise, *Lesothosaurus* had a horny beak. All ornithischian dinosaurs seem to have had beaks for snipping leaves and stems from trees and bushes.

to chew its food a little. Saurischian (lizard-hipped) dinosaurs, such as sauropods (long-necked plant-eaters) and all meat-eaters, had no cheeks. They had to swallow their food whole; it would have spilled out of their mouths if they had tried to chew it.

Beaky dinosaur

Another important feature of ornithischian dinosaurs is that they all had beaks. The beak would have covered the front parts of their upper and lower jaws. It would have been the same as the beaks modern turtles and tortoises have.

Its beak would have helped *Lesothosaurus* to bite off the leaves and soft twigs that it ate. This beak would have been

made of hardened skin, just like our fingernails. Like our fingernails, it would continue to grow throughout the animal's life. The beak would constantly wear down at the edges because of biting. However, because it kept growing, it would stay about the same length.

One further clue tells us *Lesothosaurus* was an ornithischian—it had an extra bone at the front tip of its lower jaw. This bone is seen in all ornithischian dinosaurs. Animals as different as horned *Triceratops*, duckbilled *Edmontosaurus*, and plate-backed *Stegosaurus* are all ornithischians, and they all have this extra bone forming part of their chin.

How did it live?

By looking at the differences in length between *Lesothosaurus*'s arms and legs, scientists can see

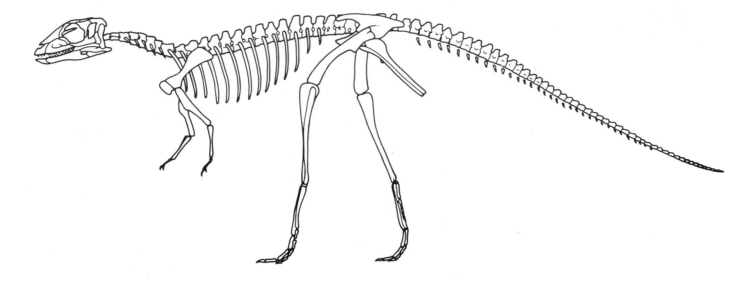

that *Lesothosaurus* was a biped—it would have spent most of its time calmly walking around on its two hind legs like a kangaroo.

Sometimes it would have gotten down on all fours. *Lesothosaurus*'s arms were very short. It would have been difficult to walk quickly on all fours with such short arms. *Lesothosaurus*'s legs were perfect for running, though. Its upper leg bone was shorter than the lower leg bone. Its feet and toes were long and slender. Only animals that need to run fast have this pattern of leg and foot bones. The ostrich, a fast-running bird, has legs and feet

like this; ornithomimosaurs (ostrichlike dinosaurs), such as *Struthiomimus*, did, too.

Fast defense

It is easy to see why little *Lesothosaurus* would have needed to run fast. It did not have sharp teeth or claws. It did not have spikes or any other type of body armor. The only way *Lesothosaurus* could protect itself would be to run away from danger.

If a hungry meat-eating dinosaur chased *Lesothosaurus*, it would have had a very hard time trying to catch it up. In Africa today, lions and cheetahs find it difficult to

▲ *Lesothosaurus* had long legs and slender feet. It was a light dinosaur and almost certainly a fast runner. Its stiff tail would have let it turn sharply at speed.

catch gazelles. Gazelles are very fast runners that are always watching and listening for danger. At the first sign of a big, hungry cat, they run for their lives. Lions and cheetahs only rarely catch a gazelle. Like the gazelles, little *Lesothosaurus* would have been constantly on the lookout for predators and would have run away as soon as one appeared.

Safety in numbers?

Like modern gazelles, *Lesothosaurus* may have lived in herds. A small dinosaur like this may have been safer if it was part of a large group. In a large group there are many more pairs of eyes watching for danger. If one *Lesothosaurus* in a herd saw danger, it could start running first. The other herd members would realize that something was wrong and start running too. This way the whole herd would be safe.

NEW BONES, NEW NAME

Lesothosaurus was originally called *Fabrosaurus* in honor of the French scientist Jean Fabre. The first *Fabrosaurus* fossil was found in 1964, but it was only a part of a jawbone with some teeth—not very useful for identifying a new dinosaur. In 1970, a team of fossil-hunters from London University and the British Museum of Natural History found a new, more complete skeleton of an animal with teeth just like those of *Fabrosaurus*. Paleontologist Tony Thulborn described the new remains, and they were named *Fabrosaurus*, too. Paleontologists then changed their minds. They thought the original 1964 fossil of *Fabrosaurus* was not good enough for identifying future dinosaurs. They renamed the new, more complete skeleton *Lesothosaurus*.

Stubby hands

Only a few *Lesothosaurus* hand and finger bones are known. However, scientists can tell that *Lesothosaurus*'s hands were short, and the fingers were not very flexible. *Lesothosaurus* could not have picked up something off the ground or held its food with its hands. It seems that *Lesothosaurus*'s teeth, jaws, and beak were its main ways of gathering food.

Like its hand, *Lesothosaurus*'s tail is poorly known. Only a few tail bones were found with the skeletons. We do know, though, that *Lesothosaurus*'s tail would have stuck straight out backward. It would never have dragged along the ground.

Rudder tail

Even at high speed, *Lesothosaurus* could have turned on a dime because its stiff tail worked like a rudder. Cheetahs use their tails like this today. *Lesothosaurus*'s tail would have helped it to balance, too. Without the weight of its tail, *Lesothosaurus* would have fallen flat on its face.

Lesothosaurus's backbones tell us it would have held its spine level while it walked. *Lesothosaurus* could have tipped up its body for a look around or to reach up for some leaves to eat, but this would not have been its normal posture.

CHECK THESE OUT!

Edmontosaurus, Hadrosaurs, Jurassic period, Ornithischian dinosaurs, Pisanosaurus, Stegosaurus, Struthiomimus, Triceratops, Tyrannosaurus, Velociraptor

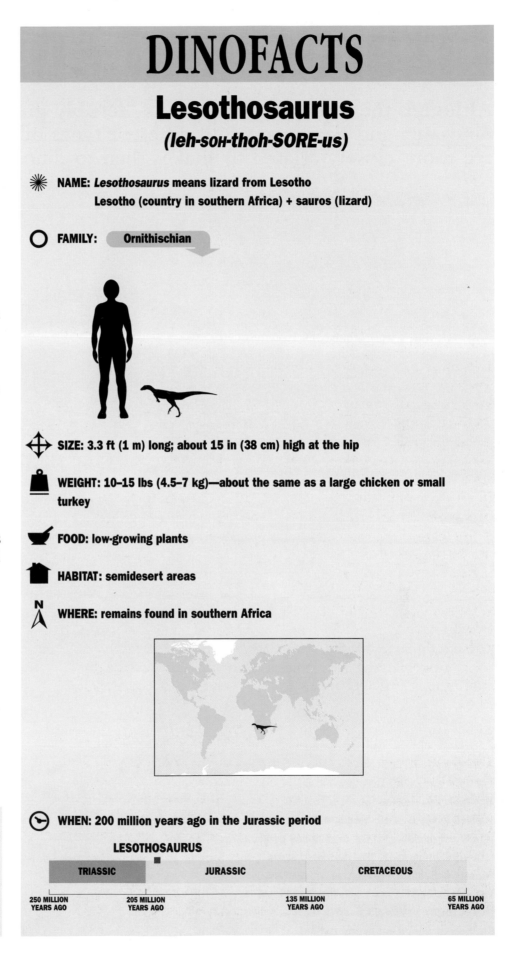

DINOFACTS

Lesothosaurus
(leh-SOH-thoh-SORE-us)

NAME: *Lesothosaurus* means lizard from Lesotho
Lesotho (country in southern Africa) + sauros (lizard)

FAMILY: Ornithischian

SIZE: 3.3 ft (1 m) long; about 15 in (38 cm) high at the hip

WEIGHT: 10–15 lbs (4.5–7 kg)—about the same as a large chicken or small turkey

FOOD: low-growing plants

HABITAT: semidesert areas

WHERE: remains found in southern Africa

WHEN: 200 million years ago in the Jurassic period

LESOTHOSAURUS

TRIASSIC	JURASSIC	CRETACEOUS
250 MILLION YEARS AGO	205 MILLION YEARS AGO	135 MILLION YEARS AGO	65 MILLION YEARS AGO

Lizards and snakes

Although the word *dinosaur* means "terribly great lizard," dinosaurs and lizards are two different types of reptiles. Lizards are more closely related to snakes than to dinosaurs.

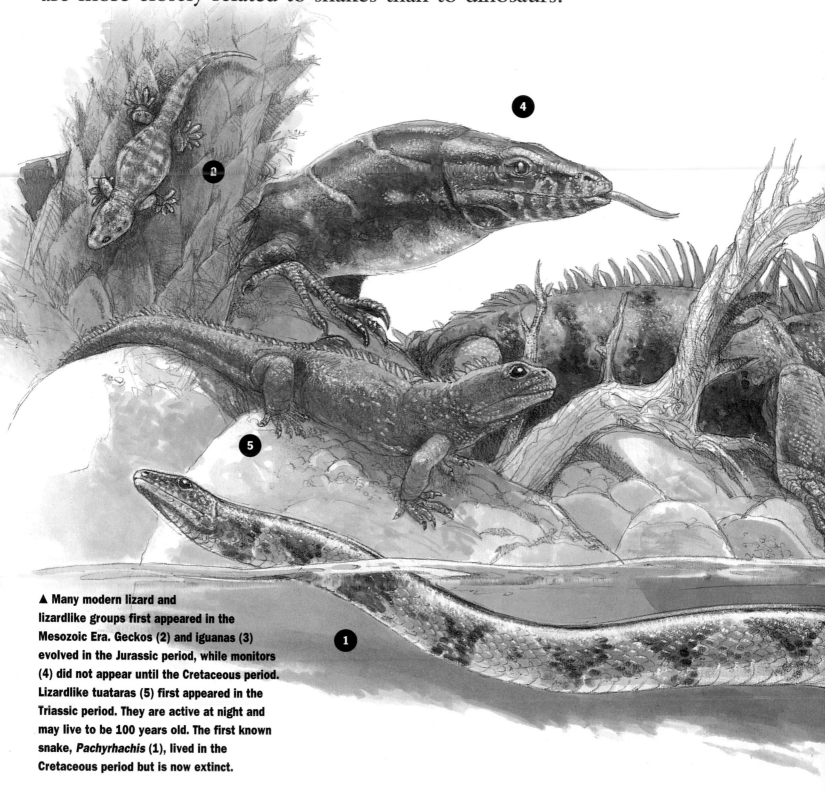

▲ Many modern lizard and lizardlike groups first appeared in the Mesozoic Era. Geckos (2) and iguanas (3) evolved in the Jurassic period, while monitors (4) did not appear until the Cretaceous period. Lizardlike tuataras (5) first appeared in the Triassic period. They are active at night and may live to be 100 years old. The first known snake, *Pachyrhachis* (1), lived in the Cretaceous period but is now extinct.

How could something like a big, slow, tree-climbing boa constrictor be related to a small, fast, ground-running *Deinonychus*? Because it is. Dinosaurs (including modern birds), lizards, and snakes are all members of a large group of animals called diapsids (animals with two pairs of openings in their skulls behind their eyes). Other members of this group are crocodiles, ancient sea-living reptiles (such as ichthyosaurs), and the extinct flying pterosaurs.

There are almost 6,000 different kinds of lizards and snakes alive today. They live

3

LIZARDS ARE NOT DINOSAURS

The nonflying dinosaurs were NOT big lizards! Dinosaurs and lizards are two different types of diapsid reptiles. Nonflying dinosaurs were archosaurs. They had openings in their skulls behind their eye sockets. While the animals were alive, the holes were covered by skin and could not be seen. Lizards belong to a different group of reptiles that no longer have holes behind their eye sockets. Dinosaurs and lizards also have different types of hips. Dinosaurs' hips let them walk with their legs tucked beneath their bodies. This allowed dinosaurs like *Brachiosaurus* to grow to huge sizes. Lizards could never grow to be as big as dinosaurs. Lizards' legs stick out sideways from their bodies, and their elbows and knees are always bent. Imagine doing push-ups all day! Lizards also twist their bodies from side to side as they walk. Dinosaurs did not. They needed stiff, strong backs to support their huge bodies.

Dinosaurs' teeth were also very different from lizards' teeth. The earliest dinosaurs, and all meat-eating dinosaurs, had their teeth set in deep sockets along the edges of their jaws. This made the teeth very strong. The animals could bite into very large prey or crunch through big bones and body armor. Lizards have teeth that are loosely fixed in their jaws. Most lizards eat smaller, less hard foods like insects.

in all types of habitats except polar regions and temperate oceans. They can be found in freshwater lakes and ponds, tropical seas, rainforests, deserts, and grasslands.

Open wide!
One of the reasons lizards have become so numerous and widespread is the design of their skulls. Lizards' skulls are very lightly built and very

flexible. For example, lizards can move their snout up and down without moving the rest of their head. Because their skulls are so flexible, they can also move their food around with their jaws to get it in the right position before they bite.

Birds have similar skulls, but most dinosaurs' skulls were completely different. They were rigid boxes of bones. Dinosaurs needed such strong skulls to grind a mouthful of tough plants or tear a lump of flesh from their thick-skinned prey. A strong bite is powered by huge jaw muscles and a very sturdy skull.

Snakes' skulls are still more flexible than lizards' skulls— even the bones in the roof of a snake's mouth can all move separately! The joint between the two halves of the lower jaw (the chin) is just a strip of soft, bendable tissue. The back of the skull can also expand sideways. The flexible jaw,

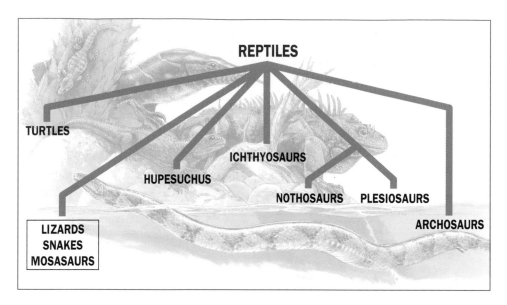

REPTILES

TURTLES

ICHTHYOSAURS

HUPESUCHUS

NOTHOSAURS   PLESIOSAURS

ARCHOSAURS

LIZARDS
SNAKES
MOSASAURS

chin, and skull let snakes swallow foods that are much wider than their heads.

The first lizards

Lizards first appeared in the Middle Jurassic period. Their fossils, sometimes found near dinosaur remains, are very rare. Their delicate skeletons would have been pounded to powder if they had been washed into a stream or stepped on. Besides, lizards usually live in dry upland areas. Carcasses rarely fossilize in these areas because there is little sand or mud to bury and protect them.

The most common lizard remains are pieces of jaw, backbones, and teeth. A few good fossils are known, but they give scientists only a tiny picture of how lizards evolved. Scientists do know that lizards developed alongside insects. Insects are a plentiful food source. It seems that as their

▶ The Komodo dragon is the world's biggest lizard, but *Megalania* from the Pleistocene period (1.8–0.5 million years ago) was even bigger at 18 ft (6 m) long.

▲ Lizards and snakes are reptiles, but they belong to a different group from the dinosaurs. Lizards and snakes are closely related to the sea-going mosasaurs. Dinosaurs belong to the archosaurs.

flexible skulls and delicate, piercing teeth evolved, lizards were better able to eat insects.

One of the best lizard fossils was found in what would have been the stomach area of the dinosaur *Compsognathus*. Paleontologists think the dinosaur ate it. They called the lizard *Bavarisaurus* in honor of

Bavaria, the area of Germany in which it was found. They think it was a fast runner, but not as fast as *Compsognathus*!

Egg-eating dragons

Paleontologists found lizard remains near the nests of *Maiasaura*, a hadrosaur, or duckbill dinosaur, that lived in Montana in the Cretaceous period. These lizards belonged to a group called the monitors. Paleontologists think lizards may have eaten *Maiasaura*'s eggs, since modern monitors eat bird and crocodile eggs.

The largest lizard today is a monitor that lives in Indonesia. The Komodo dragon grows up to 10 ft (3 m) long and can eat a whole pig at one time.

First snake

Snake fossils are even more delicate than lizard fossils, and thus even rarer. The earliest known snake was found in Early Cretaceous rocks in Israel. It is called *Pachyrhachis*, and one of its special features was that it had back legs!

Pachyrhachis seems to have been a water snake. Perhaps it used its tiny legs as rudders to help keep it on course as it swam.

Paleontologists think snakes evolved from lizards closely related to the monitors. Even today, both monitors and snakes have long, low skulls on long, flexible necks. One very important feature that snakes and monitors share is a long, forked tongue. Snakes and monitors often stick out their tongues to "taste" the air. Their forked tongues are doing the same job as our noses when we sniff the air.

Lizard vs. snake

There are many differences between lizards and snakes, too. Lizards have legs, eyelids, external ears, and can see in color. Snakes have no legs, no eyelids, no external ears, and can see only in black and white. They lost these features and abilities as they evolved.

However, snakes have developed some awesome abilities. Whereas lizards evolved alongside insects, it seems snakes evolved alongside small mammals. One group of snakes, the rattlesnakes and vipers, have developed special heat detectors on their snouts. These help the snakes find mice and rats in the dark by sensing their body heat.

CHECK THESE OUT!

Archosaurs, Birds, *Brachiosaurus*, *Compsognathus*, Cretaceous period, Dinosaurs, Ichthyosaurs, Insects, Jurassic period, *Maiasaura*, Mammals, Pterosaurs, Reptiles

FOSSIL FACTS

Lizards and snakes

▶ Fossil-hunters found this skeleton in Germany. Little *Ardeosaurus* was an 8 in (20 cm) gecko and one of the earliest known lizards.

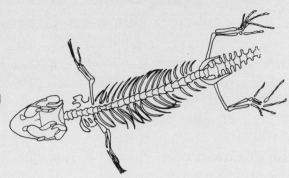

○ **FAMILY:** Reptile

 SIZE: (includes prehistoric and modern) lizards—1 in (2.5 cm) to 18 ft (6 m); snakes—4 in (10 cm) to 30 ft (9 m) or more

 FOOD: lizards—varies, from insects to meat or plants; snakes—meat, fish, insects

 HABITAT: varies, from deserts to forests to swamps to warm seas

 WHERE: worldwide except for polar regions and temperate oceans

WHEN: lizards—160 million years ago in the Jurassic period to today; snakes—140 million years ago in the Cretaceous period to today

LIZARDS AND SNAKES

TRIASSIC	JURASSIC	CRETACEOUS
250 MILLION YEARS AGO	205 MILLION YEARS AGO	135 MILLION YEARS AGO / 65 MILLION YEARS AGO

Lufengosaurus

Lufengosaurus was a prosauropod, an ancestor of the long-necked, long-tailed plant-eaters called sauropods. This dinosaur's name refers to the fossil-rich place in China where it was discovered.

Chinese paleontologist C. C. Young described *Lufengosaurus* in 1941. The dinosaur was first discovered in some purplish-red mudstones known as the Lufeng Formation, in China.

Paleontologists have found a wealth of fossil remains in Lufeng—amphibians, crocodiles, mammal-like reptiles, and small, primitive (little evolved) mammals.

Other dinosaurs discovered at Lufeng include the stegosaur (plate-backed dinosaur) *Tatisaurus* and the theropod (two-legged meat-eater) *Dilophosaurus*.

Lufengosaurus is one of many prosauropods (ancestors of sauropods) found at Lufeng; others include *Yunnanosaurus* and *Anchisaurus*. Some paleontologists think that most

of the Lufeng prosauropods are just different examples of the same dinosaur. However, there are differences in the age of the fossils and in the size and form of some of their bones. These differences suggest to other scientists that the prosauropods really are different kinds. *Lufengosaurus* could well be closely related to *Plateosaurus* from Germany.

▼ Long-necked and long-tailed, *Lufengosaurus* was an Early Jurassic prosauropod, an ancestor of the mighty sauropods.

DINOFACTS

Lufengosaurus
(loo-FUNG-guh-SORE-us)

✳ **NAME:** *Lufengosaurus* means Lufeng lizard
Lufeng (place in China) + sauros (lizard)

○ **FAMILY:**
- Saurischian
  - Sauropodomorph
    - Prosauropod

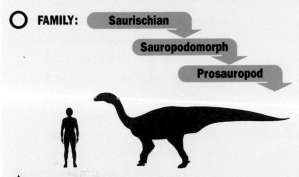

✥ **SIZE:** 20 ft (6 m) long; 7 ft (2.1 m) high at the hip

⚖ **WEIGHT:** 5–10 tons (4.5–9 tonnes)—about the same as 1–2 African elephants

🥣 **FOOD:** plants

🏠 **HABITAT:** low-lying, leafy plains

⇡ **WHERE:** remains found in China

▶ *Lufengosaurus* had small, jagged teeth. It probably used them to snip off plant food.

🕐 **WHEN:** 205–200 million years ago in the Jurassic period

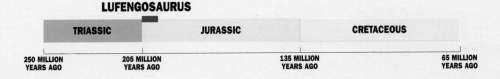

LUFENGOSAURUS

TRIASSIC	JURASSIC	CRETACEOUS
250 MILLION YEARS AGO	205 MILLION YEARS AGO	135 MILLION YEARS AGO	65 MILLION YEARS AGO

TWO LEGS OR FOUR?

Like all prosauropods, *Lufengosaurus* had much longer back legs than front legs. This suggests that *Lufengosaurus* might sometimes have stood up on its back legs, just as it was first shown in Chinese museums. Standing on its back legs, *Lufengosaurus* could have reached up and eaten foliage from the tops of tall trees. When walking or running, though, *Lufengosaurus* might have used all four of its legs. Its long neck and body would probably have made it difficult for the dinosaur to keep its balance while moving around only on its back legs.

In 1958, *Lufengosaurus* became the first ever Chinese dinosaur to have its complete skeleton displayed in a museum. China celebrated the event by issuing a postage stamp showing the skeleton.

How *Lufengosaurus* lived

Like other prosauropods, *Lufengosaurus* had small, widely spaced teeth with jagged edges. Scientists think it used these teeth to eat plants, but they are not sure. However, they point out that because prosauropods are the most common fossils in Lufeng, they must have been plant-eaters. Plant-eaters are more common than meat-eaters in any food chain; otherwise there would not be enough of them for the meat-eaters to eat! We see this today in Africa, where plant-eating zebra and antelope are more common than lions or hyenas.

CHECK THESE OUT!

Amphibians, *Anchisaurus*, Crocodiles, *Dilophosaurus*, Jurassic period, Mammal-like reptiles, Mammals, *Plateosaurus*, Prosauropods, Rocks, Saurischian dinosaurs, Sauropods, Theropods

Maiasaura

The discovery of *Maiasaura* is one of the most exciting dinosaur finds of all time. It revealed to paleontologists for the first time that dinosaurs may have actively looked after their young.

American paleontologist Jack Horner dug up an adult hadrosaur (duckbill dinosaur) in Montana in 1979. With it were the skeletons of 11 baby hadrosaurs. The babies were near a dishlike dip in the rock. Scientists believe this dip was a dinosaur nest. Nearby were several bits of fossil eggshells, so scientists could tell the babies had already hatched.

Since 1979, paleontologists have found many fossils of *Maiasaura*, as the dinosaur became known. There are lots of complete skeletons of animals of different ages, so that scientists can see how *Maiasaura* grew and developed.

Solid crest

Maiasaura's skull was broad at the front, with a wide, bill-like mouth. It had a crest on its head—not a big, hollow one like many hadrosaurs, but a low, solid ridge. *Maiasaura* had strong back legs and smaller front limbs; this suggested to

GOOD MOTHER

Maiasaura means good mother lizard. Horner gave the dinosaur this name because it seemed that the adult *Maiasaura* cared for its babies. Why do scientists think this? Some of the babies Horner found were newly hatched; others were up to a month old. Because the older babies had stayed in the nest, one or both parents must have brought food to them. Perhaps the parents also protected their nestbound babies from predators.

344

scientists that the dinosaur sometimes moved on its back legs. *Maiasaura* also had a long tail. Perhaps it used its tail like a rudder when it ran so it could turn quickly.

How *Maiasaura* lived

Some scientists think *Maiasaura* moved from place to place depending on the time of year. For example, zebra and wildebeest migrate today on the African plains.

For part of the year, the dinosaurs lived in leafy areas. Once a year they returned to river floodplains to lay their eggs. Each mother scraped a hollow in the dirt to use as a nest. She laid the oval-shaped eggs in the nest. She may have covered the eggs in rotting leaves to keep them warm.

◀ It seems *Maiasaura* looked after its babies. Scientists do not know when young *Maiasaura* started to look after themselves.

CHECK THESE OUT!
Cretaceous period, Digging dinosaurs, Eggs and babies, Hadrosaurs, Ornithischian dinosaurs

DINOFACTS

Maiasaura
(MY-uh-SORE-uh)

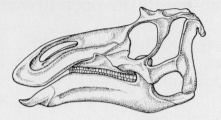

▶ *Maiasaura* was a hadrosaur, but unlike many hadrosaurs it did not have a large crest on the top of its head—just a low ridge.

✸ **NAME:** *Maiasaura* means good mother lizard
maia (good mother) + saura (lizard)

○ **FAMILY:** Ornithischian
⟶ Ornithopod
⟶ Hadrosaur

✦ **SIZE:** 37 ft (11.3 m) long; 12 ft (3.6 m) high at the hip

⚖ **WEIGHT:** 4–7 tons (3.6–6.3 tonnes)—about the same as 4–7 North American bison

⊻ **FOOD:** plants

⌂ **HABITAT:** dry lowland plains

↑N **WHERE:** remains found in Montana

⏱ **WHEN:** 77–73 million years ago in the Cretaceous period

			MAIASAURA
TRIASSIC	JURASSIC	CRETACEOUS	■
250 MILLION YEARS AGO	205 MILLION YEARS AGO	135 MILLION YEARS AGO	65 MILLION YEARS AGO

Majungatholus

A recent discovery has revealed much about this mysterious predator. *Majungatholus* was the largest theropod (two-legged meat-eater) known from the Late Cretaceous period of Madagascar.

Majungatholus has a confusing history. The first specimens of the dinosaur we now call *Majungatholus* were some teeth and some bones from the lower jaw. Fossil-hunters found them in Madagascar, a large island off the east coast of Africa. French paleontologist Charles Depéret thought they were the bones of *Megalosaurus*, a big meat-eating dinosaur. In the 1950s, though, French paleontologist René Lavocat realized the bones were not from *Megalosaurus*. He renamed the dinosaur *Majungasaurus*.

Dome head

In the early 1900s, fossil-hunters had found some other skull bones near *Majungasaurus*. These were long ignored, until paleontologists Hans-Dieter Sues and Phillipe Taquet re-examined them in the late

NAME CALLING

Majungatholus has been called by three different names: *Megalosaurus*, *Majungasaurus*, and *Majungatholus*. How do scientists choose which name to use? Although *Majungatholus* was first thought to be a new kind (species) of *Megalosaurus*, studies of its bones showed that it was too different from *Megalosaurus* to keep that name. That is why it got the new name *Majungasaurus*. However, when US paleontologist Scott Sampson and colleagues showed that *Majungasaurus* and *Majungatholus* were the same dinosaur, they had to choose which name to use. According to the rules, the earliest name given to a dinosaur is considered the correct name. So paleontologists chose *Majungasaurus* for the Madagascan dinosaur, since the name was 24 years older than *Majungatholus*. In the 1990s, paleontologists decided to break the rules. They renamed the dinosaur *Majungatholus* because this name more accurately described the dome-headed meat-eater.

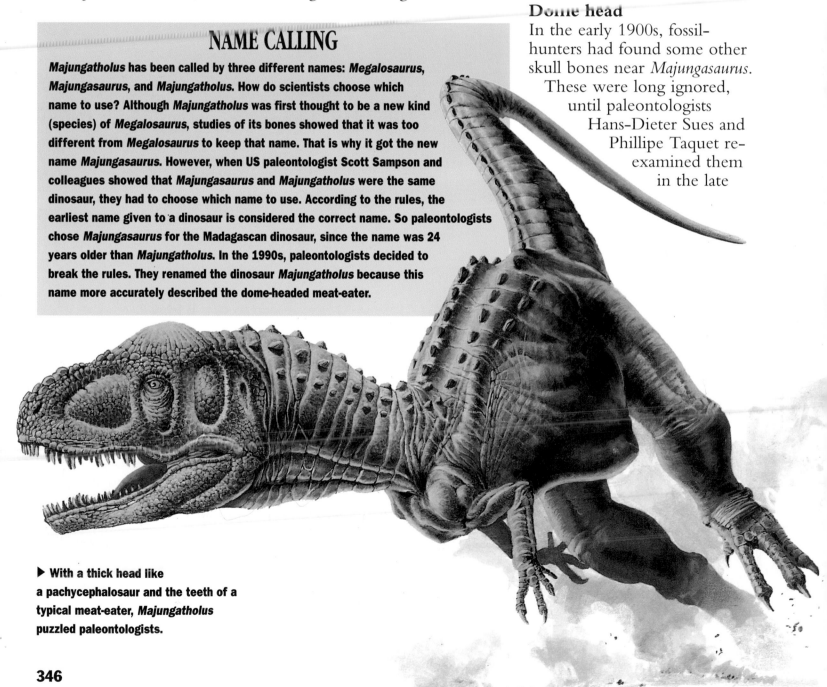

▶ With a thick head like a pachycephalosaur and the teeth of a typical meat-eater, *Majungatholus* puzzled paleontologists.

1970s. Because the bones were so thick, they thought they belonged to the skull of a new kind of pachycephalosaur (thick-headed dinosaur). They named it *Majungatholus*.

Dome head, dagger teeth

In the 1990s, paleontologists found a complete dinosaur skull in Madagascar. It had the same jaw as *Majungasaurus* and the same top as *Majungatholus*. Guess what! *Majungasaurus* and *Majungatholus* were the same kind of dinosaur! For some years, scientists continued to call the dinosaur *Majungasaurus*.

In the late 1990s, though, paleontologists changed their minds and began to call it *Majungatholus* instead.

Majungatholus was not a pachycephalosaur but a ceratosaur, a four-fingered meat-eating dinosaur related to *Ceratosaurus*, *Abelisaurus*, and *Carnotaurus*. It was the only kind of meat-eating dinosaur with a domed head.

How did it live?

Like other ceratosaurs, *Majungatholus* ate meat. It hunted the Late Cretaceous forests of Madagascar, looking

for dinosaurs to kill or the carcasses of already dead dinosaurs to scavenge.

Majungatholus may have used its dome in displays to warn off other dinosaurs or to attract mates. It may also have used its dome to push against other dinosaurs of its kind in contests over territory, food, or mates.

CHECK THESE OUT!

Abelisaurus, Carnotaurus, Ceratosaurs, Ceratosaurus, Cretaceous period, Megalosaurus, Pachycephalosaurs, Saurischian dinosaurs, Theropods

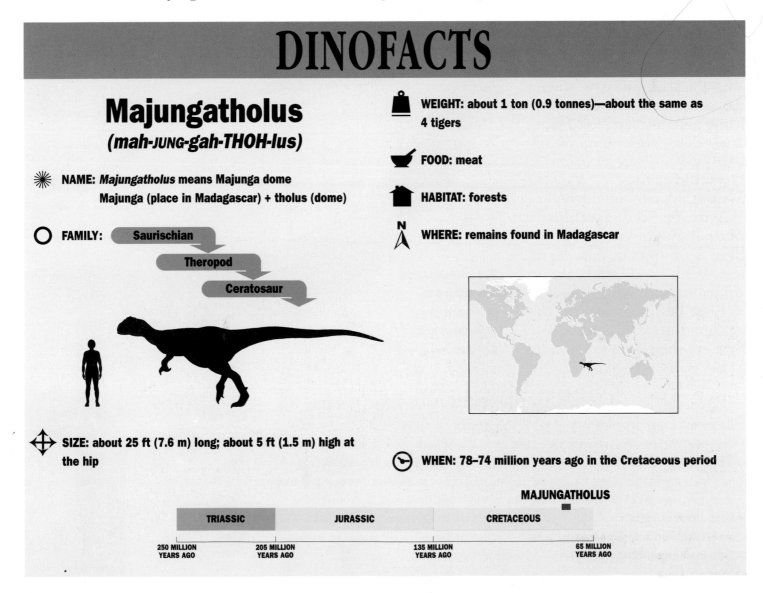

DINOFACTS

Majungatholus
(mah-JUNG-gah-THOH-lus)

☀ NAME: *Majungatholus* means Majunga dome
Majunga (place in Madagascar) + tholus (dome)

○ FAMILY: Saurischian → Theropod → Ceratosaur

⚖ WEIGHT: about 1 ton (0.9 tonnes)—about the same as 4 tigers

FOOD: meat

HABITAT: forests

WHERE: remains found in Madagascar

✦ SIZE: about 25 ft (7.6 m) long; about 5 ft (1.5 m) high at the hip

🕐 WHEN: 78–74 million years ago in the Cretaceous period

TRIASSIC	JURASSIC	CRETACEOUS	MAJUNGATHOLUS
250 MILLION YEARS AGO	205 MILLION YEARS AGO	135 MILLION YEARS AGO	65 MILLION YEARS AGO

Mamenchisaurus

Sauropod dinosaurs are famous for their long necks, but one sauropod had a neck that was more than half its total body length! Named *Mamenchisaurus*, it lived in China in the Jurassic period.

Chinese paleontologist C.C. Young named this dinosaur when he described its fossil remains in 1954. Of a total body length of up to 82 ft (25 m), *Mamenchisaurus* could have had a 50 ft (15.2 m) neck. From the Late Triassic period to the end of the Cretaceous, different groups of sauropods evolved very long necks. These adaptations gave them special advantages, such as being able to reach food that other dinosaurs could not.

How did it live?

Mamenchisaurus could have used its super-long neck to eat all the low-growing plants in a large field without moving its feet. With a long neck, the animal did not have to move its huge body much—just its head and neck. It could also have reached up into tall trees.

Sometimes having a long neck can be a hassle. Your heart has to pump really hard to get your blood all the way up to your head. Modern giraffes have necks about 10 ft (3 m) long. They have extra muscles in their necks to help to squeeze the blood up to their heads. They also have a

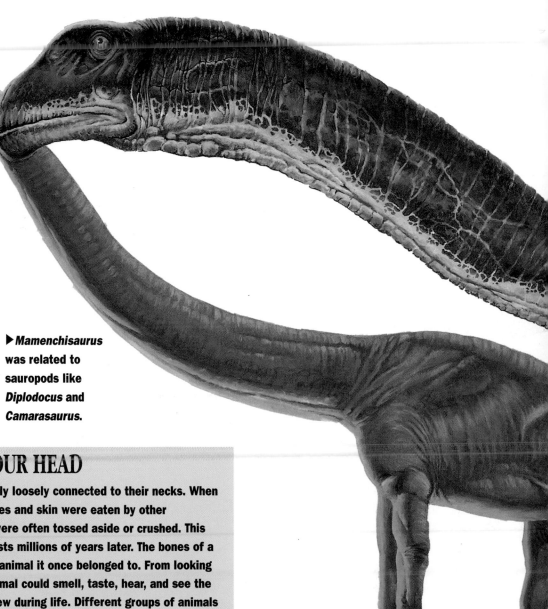

▶*Mamenchisaurus* was related to sauropods like *Diplodocus* and *Camarasaurus*.

LOSING YOUR HEAD

Sauropods seem to have had their heads only loosely connected to their necks. When they died, their bodies rotted or their muscles and skin were eaten by other dinosaurs. Like animals today, their heads were often tossed aside or crushed. This has caused great problems for paleontologists millions of years later. The bones of a skull contain a lot of information about the animal it once belonged to. From looking at its skull, scientists can learn how the animal could smell, taste, hear, and see the world. The skull can show how an animal grew during life. Different groups of animals have their skull bones and jawbones arranged differently.

heart the size of a basketball. No one knows how *Mamenchisaurus* managed.

Message to brain

Another problem with a really long neck is getting messages between the brain and the rest of the body. Nerves from the brain carry signals to muscles in the arms, legs, and tail. Think how long it would take for nerves in *Mamenchisaurus*'s foot to feel pain, signal the brain, then have the brain send a message to tell the leg muscles to move the foot.

CHECK THESE OUT!

Camarasaurus, Cretaceous period, *Diplodocus*, Jurassic period, Saurischian dinosaurs, Sauropods, Triassic period

DINOFACTS

Mamenchisaurus
(ma-MEN-chee-SORE-us)

▶ **Mamenchisaurus** is the largest dinosaur ever found in Asia and has the longest neck of any dinosaur.

✳ **NAME:** *Mamenchisaurus* means lizard from Mamen Brook
Mamen (name of stream) + chi (brook) + sauros (lizard)

○ **FAMILY:** Saurischian
→ Sauropodomorph
→ Sauropod

✛ **SIZE:** 82 ft (25 m) long; 15–18 ft (4.6–5.4 m) high at the hip

⚖ **WEIGHT:** 10–40 tons (9–36 tonnes)—about the same as 2–8 African elephants

🥣 **FOOD:** plants

🏠 **HABITAT:** lowland open forest

N **WHERE:** remains found in China

🕐 **WHEN:** 160 million years ago in the Jurassic period

MAMENCHISAURUS

TRIASSIC	JURASSIC	CRETACEOUS
250 MILLION YEARS AGO	205 MILLION YEARS AGO 135 MILLION YEARS AGO	65 MILLION YEARS AGO

Mammal-like reptiles

Most people have seen pictures of *Dimetrodon*, an animal with a tall sail on its back and big teeth. Most people think it was a dinosaur, but it was more closely related to humans than to dinosaurs!

Dimetrodon was a mammal-like reptile, or synapsid—an animal with only a single pair of openings, or windows, in the skull behind its eyes. Mammal-like reptiles were the ancestors of the mammals, such as cats, dogs, and humans.

Mammals are usually covered in fur or hair; female mammals produce milk to feed their babies. Mammals are also warm-blooded, which means they can control their own body temperature.

Reptiles are scaly-skinned and cold blooded. They cannot control their own body temperature and they rely on the sun to warm up. Reptiles also cannot produce milk.

Mammal-like reptiles were halfway between reptiles and mammals. They may have had hair covering their bodies, they may have produced milk for feeding their young, and they may even have been warm-blooded.

Not dinosaurs

Three things tell scientists that *Dimetrodon* and its mammal-like reptile cousins were not dinosaurs. The first is that they were synapsids. Dinosaurs were diapsids—they had two pairs of openings behind their eyes. No one knows for sure what they did, but they may have helped to make the skull lighter.

The second feature about *Dimetrodon* is the way that the skull attaches to the spinal column. In dinosaurs, the back of the skull joins the spinal column in a single bony bump. In *Dimetrodon* the skull and spinal column are joined by two smaller bony bumps, just like in mammals.

THE GREATEST EXTINCTION OF THEM ALL

The extinction at the end of the Permian period (250 million years ago) was the biggest ever. Perhaps 95 percent of the animal and plant kinds died out, including most of the mammal-like reptiles. Why? At this time, the continents joined together to form the supercontinent Pangaea. The formation of one, huge landmass caused two major changes. First, there was now much less coastline. Most sea animals live in shallow coastal waters. Too many creatures now tried to share too little habitat, so many sea animals became extinct. Climate changes also took place. Coastal areas usually have a mild, wet climate. Inland, summers are hotter and drier, while the winters are colder. Since the continents were joined, there were huge inland areas away from the oceans. The weather was harsher here than land animals had been used to. Many probably could not cope with these conditions and became extinct.

▼ Mammal-like reptiles included some strange creatures. A pack of meat-eating *Cynognathus* (1) move in on a plant-eating *Kannemeyeria* (2). Two *Lystrosaurus* (3), also plant-eaters, watch as a *Thrinaxodon* (4) eats an *Ericiolacerta*. Far away, some *Euparkeria* (5) pass by. *Euparkeria* was not a mammal-like reptile; it was an early archosaur, a relative of the dinosaurs.

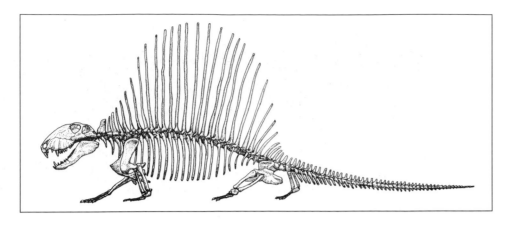

◀ *Dimetrodon* was a meat-eater 13 ft (4 m) long. The long bones sticking up from its back were covered in skin to form a sail. No one knows what the sail did.

The third feature is that all of a dinosaur's teeth were usually the same shape and size. *Dimetrodon*'s jaws contained different types of teeth. Modern mammals also have mouths full of different shapes and sizes of teeth. Each tooth type does a different job.

A cat, for example, which is a meat-eater, has snipping teeth at the front of its mouth. Behind these are long, stabbing (canine) teeth. Behind these are sharp-edged, triangular teeth for slicing up chunks of meat. A sheep, which eats plants, has square-edged lower front teeth and a bony upper pad for grasping and tearing up grass. Behind these, its cheeks have broad, flat teeth for grinding its food to a pulp before swallowing. Some mammal-like reptiles ate only meat, some ate only plants, and some ate both meat and plants. Some even ate fish.

Animals of the Permian

The mammal-like reptiles first appeared about 320 million years ago in the Carboniferous period (360–290 million years ago). During the Permian period (290–250 million years ago) they became the most common land animals. Mammal-like reptile fossils have been found all over the world—in India, South America, North America, Europe, Africa, Australia, and Antarctica. Two places are especially important—Texas and South Africa. Each of these places records the evolution of mammal-like reptiles at different times.

Texan meat-eater

Dimetrodon was a meat-eating mammal-like reptile found in Texas rocks that date from the

Late Carboniferous to the Early Permian periods (300–260 million years ago). It shared its swampy world with other mammal-like reptiles like plant-eating *Edaphosaurus*.

Dimetrodon and *Edaphosaurus* both had sails on their backs. Some scientists think these sails helped the animals cool down or warm up more quickly. Elephants today use their big ears like this. However, other scientists point out that most mammal-like reptiles did not have sails on their backs, so how did they control their body temperatures?

South African plant-eaters

Later in the Permian, many new kinds of mammal-like reptiles evolved. Among the most common of these were the dicynodonts (meaning "two dog-teeth"). They first appeared in the Late Permian period, in South Africa.

▶ Along with mammals, the mammal-like reptiles belonged to the group of animals called synapsids.

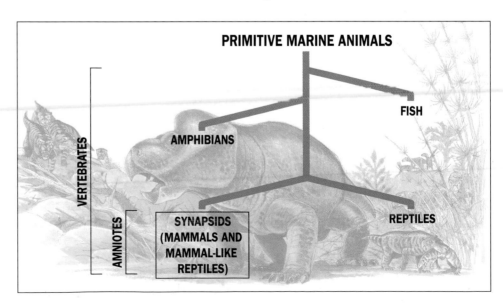

PRIMITIVE MARINE ANIMALS

VERTEBRATES

AMNIOTES

AMPHIBIANS

FISH

SYNAPSIDS (MAMMALS AND MAMMAL-LIKE REPTILES)

REPTILES

Dicynodonts had only two tusks in their upper jaw and no other teeth. They did have a beaklike covering on their snouts, though, just like a turtle. Dicynodonts ate plants. They would have used their tusks to dig up roots. Their sharp beaks would have helped bite off leaves and stems.

By the Early Triassic period, the dicynodonts had become very numerous. *Lystrosaurus* was a common dicynodont. Thousands of its fossil remains have been found. *Lystrosaurus* was about 3 ft (about 90 cm) long and lived near the shores of large lakes.

While dicynodonts munched on plants, early saber-toothed meat-eaters stalked. Saber-tooths could open their lower jaw very wide, exposing the huge canine teeth they used for grabbing and stabbing prey. Long-legged *Lycaenops* was an early saber-tooth. It was about the same size as *Lystrosaurus*.

Almost mammals

The cynodonts were a group of mammal-like reptiles that included the ancestors of the true mammals. Like modern mammals, they had a mixture of snipping teeth, canine teeth, and cheek teeth. *Thrinaxodon* lived in South Africa in the Early Triassic. Scientists think it was warm-blooded and could breathe while eating, like a modern mammal.

Like mammals, *Thrinaxodon* had a layer of bone in the roof of its mouth. This layer let air in through the nose and to the back of the throat. Reptiles do not have this layer. They have

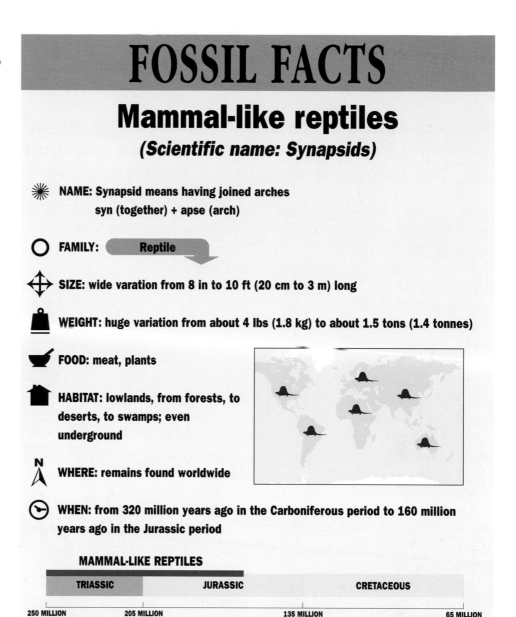

FOSSIL FACTS

Mammal-like reptiles
(Scientific name: Synapsids)

NAME: Synapsid means having joined arches
syn (together) + apse (arch)

FAMILY: Reptile

SIZE: wide varation from 8 in to 10 ft (20 cm to 3 m) long

WEIGHT: huge variation from about 4 lbs (1.8 kg) to about 1.5 tons (1.4 tonnes)

FOOD: meat, plants

HABITAT: lowlands, from forests, to deserts, to swamps; even underground

WHERE: remains found worldwide

WHEN: from 320 million years ago in the Carboniferous period to 160 million years ago in the Jurassic period

MAMMAL-LIKE REPTILES

TRIASSIC	JURASSIC	CRETACEOUS
250 MILLION YEARS AGO	205 MILLION YEARS AGO · 135 MILLION YEARS AGO	65 MILLION YEARS AGO

to stop breathing when they eat. Because of this layer of bone, mammals can breathe even when they are eating.

End of the line

In the middle of the Triassic period, when the dinosaurs appeared, the mammal-like reptiles began to disappear. Scientists believe changes took place in climate and plant life at this time. Perhaps the mammal-like reptiles could not cope with them. By the end of

the Triassic period, the larger mammal-like reptiles had vanished. The smaller ones lost out to the mammals, which had more efficient teeth and jaws. By the Middle Jurassic period, all the mammal-like reptiles were gone.

CHECK THESE OUT!

Archosaurs, Continental drift, Dinosaurs, Extinction, Geological time, Jurassic period, Mammals, Reptiles, Triassic period

Mammals

Tiny mammals were already scampering about the feet of the first dinosaurs in the Mesozoic Era. When the nonflying dinosaurs died out, the mammals took over. Today, we live in the age of mammals.

Mammals are the ruling large animals on earth today. They range in size from the teaspoon-sized least shrew to the blue whale at 100 ft (30 m) long and 95 tons (86 tonnes).

Mammals live in nearly every habitat on land, plus a few in the air and sea. For example, bats fly, while whales and sea cows live only in the water. Modern mammals are divided into 21 large groups with nearly 4,500 individual kinds (species).

All mammals have hair or fur and produce milk to feed their young. Nearly all give birth to live young, with the exception of the platypus and echidna, which lay eggs. The platypus is a small, duckbilled Australian animal that spends much of its life in water. The echidna, or spiny anteater, looks a little like a porcupine and lives in Australia and on the nearby island of New Guinea.

Drawing the line
Mammals evolved from the mammal-like reptiles. However, the evolution was so gradual that scientists have not generally agreed on where to draw the line between mammal-like reptile and mammal.

One major difference between modern mammals and their ancestors is in their ears. Modern mammals have three bones in their inner ear; all other land-living animals had (and have) only one. These extra ear bones originally linked mammals' jaws to their skulls.

▼ Cretaceous mammals *Deltatheridium* (1), insect-eating *Barunlestes* (2), and squirrel-like *Nemegtbataar* (3) keep out of a hungry *Velociraptor*'s way.

Classifying mammals

Today scientists have a new way of looking at evolution to classify animals. A group of animals now includes the common ancestor and all of its descendants. For example, to know which animals are mammals you have to trace all the way back to the very first mammal, or at least as far as you can. This system is difficult to use for all mammals. Scientists do not yet understand how platypuses and echidnas first evolved.

The first mammals

Mammals first appeared either just before or just after the dinosaurs did in the Late

ROLE MODELS

By studying how modern mammals behave, scientists can make guesses about how the dinosaurs lived. Maybe sauropods (long-necked plant-eaters, such as *Apatosaurus*) lived as giraffes do. Perhaps ceratopsians (horned dinosaurs, such as *Triceratops*) lived like cattle and rhinoceroses do now. Maybe hadrosaurs (duckbill dinosaurs) lived like deer and antelope still do.

Maryland paleontologist Tom Holtz thinks that perhaps larger theropods (two-legged meat-eaters), such as *Allosaurus*, were replaced by wild dogs, and that cats replaced dromaeosaurs, such as *Velociraptor*.

Of course, modern mammals and Mesozoic dinosaurs are too different to have behaved exactly alike. Because we cannot study dinosaur behavior at first hand, we can only guess how they must have really lived.

Triassic period. These first mammals were all very tiny. Their pointed teeth tell us that they probably ate insects. Pointed teeth can be useful for puncturing and chopping up crunchy insects. Many different kinds of insect-eaters evolved, among them *Megazostrodon*. *Megazostrodon* was about 4 in (10 cm) long and was probably one of the earliest mammals.

The seed crushers

The insect-eaters were soon joined by the small rodentlike seed-collectors, the multi-tuberculates. This group of squirrel-like mammals got their name from the shape of their teeth. Their teeth had lots of little bumps, or tubercles, on them for crushing seeds.

Mammals miss out

If mammals and dinosaurs appeared at the same time, why did the dinosaurs become the ruling animals on earth? Ankles! The dinosaurs' ankles helped them to walk with their legs held under their body. This ability allowed dinosaurs to grow to huge sizes. Early mammals could not walk with their legs held under their bodies. Their ankles were floppy and could not support big, heavy animals. Dinosaurs became the large land animals of the Mesozoic Era, while mammals stayed small.

Until recently, the mammals that lived in the Mesozoic Era were known from just a few bits of bone. This is because

▶ Like mammal-like reptiles, mammals are synapsids, animals with one pair of openings in their skulls behind their eyes.

they were small and their delicate bones were easily crushed. Small fossils are also harder to find.

Collectors have found many mammal fossils in the southwestern US and Asia's Gobi Desert. From these finds, scientists see that in the Mesozoic Era there were at

least as many types of mammals as there were types of dinosaurs. Not only that, there were probably many more individual mammals than there were individual dinosaurs. This is not surprising. There seem to have been very few really small dinosaurs, and small animals always far outnumber large animals. An area can support only a limited number of large animals because they need so much to eat. The same area can hold many more small animals because they eat less.

A day in the life

Mesozoic mammals ate insects and seeds. Like most modern mammals, they were probably active mainly at night, when their fur kept them warm.

Most mammals are color-blind. The part of the eye used for color vision needs bright light to work; the part used for black-and-white vision works

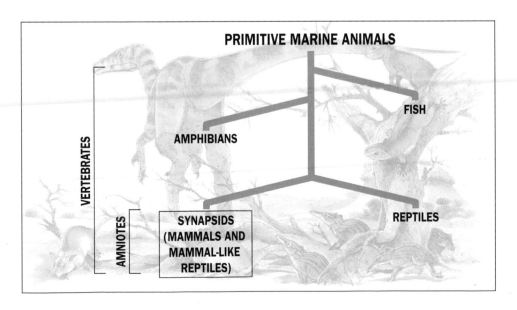

PRIMITIVE MARINE ANIMALS

VERTEBRATES

AMNIOTES

AMPHIBIANS

FISH

SYNAPSIDS (MAMMALS AND MAMMAL-LIKE REPTILES)

REPTILES

in low light. Because most mammals are mainly active at night, the color-vision area of their eye has shrunk, making them color-blind. Humans can see in color. Scientists think that in primates, such as apes and people, only those that evolved color vision, and so could find ripe fruit, survived.

Mammals and extinction

The mass extinction that wiped out the nonflying dinosaurs at the end of the Cretaceous period killed off some mammals, too. Most kinds survived, though, and paleontologists believe that mammals had a better chance of surviving because they were small. Perhaps they could find food in tiny cracks into which larger animals, including dinosaurs, could not reach.

The mammals that vanished included two groups of small marsupials, the pediomyids and the stagodontids. Marsupials are mammals that give birth to very tiny, helpless young that they rear in pouches. Modern marsupials include kangaroos and opossums.

Mammals on the move

The extinction of the nonflying dinosaurs opened up space for many different kinds of mammals to evolve. Of course, the mammals did not take over right away. It took about 10 million years for the first mammal to evolve that weighed as much as a ton. The first really big mammals were probably the plant-eating pantodonts, some of which were as big as rhinoceroses.

Mammals also evolved to fill roles not filled by dinosaurs. For example, whales and seals took over from marine reptiles such as ichthyosaurs and plesiosaurs. Bats replaced the flying reptiles, the pterosaurs.

FOSSIL FACTS

Mammals

NAME: Mammals get their name from the milk-producing (mammary) glands that all modern mammals have

◄ *Megazostrodon* lived in Africa in the Early Jurassic period. It was about as big as a mouse.

 SIZE: huge variation from less than 2 in (5 cm) to 100 ft (30 m) long; from 1 in (2.5 cm) to 18 ft (5.4 m) high

 WEIGHT: huge variation from less than 0.2 oz (6 g) to 95 tons (86 tonnes)

 FOOD: plants (including nectar and bark), meat, fish, insects

 HABITAT: varies, from forests to deserts to oceans to cities

WHERE: remains found worldwide

 WHEN: from 225 million years ago in the Triassic period to today

MAMMALS

TRIASSIC	JURASSIC	CRETACEOUS
250 MILLION YEARS AGO	205 MILLION YEARS AGO	135 MILLION YEARS AGO	65 MILLION YEARS AGO

CHECK THESE OUT!

Birds, Ceratopsians, Crocodiles, Dinosaurs, Dromaeosaurs, Eggs and babies, Evolution, Extinction, Mammal-like reptiles, Ornithopods, Pterosaurs, Sauropods, Theropods, *Triceratops*

357

Maniraptors

Birds and their closest dinosaur relatives form a group called the maniraptors. Unlike other dinosaurs, they could fold their hands out of the way against their bodies as they ran.

By studying *Dromaeosaurus*, Yale University paleontologist John Ostrom proved that birds descended from small meat-eating dinosaurs called coelurosaurs. In the 1970s, Ostrom showed that coelurosaurs and birds shared many features that no other creatures had.

In the early 1980s, Yale's Jacques Gauthier listed all the features shared by birds and other dinosaurs. His study showed not only that birds evolved from dinosaurs, but that some coelurosaurs were more closely related to birds than to other coelurosaurs. For example, dromaeosaurs (clawed meat-eaters), like *Velociraptor*, and oviraptorosaurs (egg-thief dinosaurs), such as *Oviraptor*, were more closely related to birds than to ornithomimosaurs (ostrichlike dinosaurs), such as *Struthiomimus*.

Utahraptor

Archaeopteryx

◀ **Maniraptors varied from the early avialan (bird relative) *Archaeopteryx* to *Utahraptor*, the largest of the dromaeosaurs (clawed meat-eaters).**

Maniraptors
(MAN-ee-RAP-tors)

 NAME: Maniraptor means hand snatcher
manus (hand) + raptor (snatcher, thief)

FAMILY:

- Saurischian
- Theropod
- Tetanuran

 SIZE: huge variation from the 2.3 in (5.8 cm) bee hummingbird of today to the 20 ft (6.5 m) *Utahraptor*

 WEIGHT: huge variation from about 0.06 oz (1.6 g) to about 1,000 lbs (454 kg)

 FOOD: varies, from plants to insects to meat

 HABITAT: wide variation, from deserts to swamps and oceans

 WHERE: remains found worldwide

WHEN: from about 165 million years ago in the Jurassic period to today (because birds are maniraptors)

MANIRAPTORS

TRIASSIC	JURASSIC	CRETACEOUS
250 MILLION YEARS AGO	205 MILLION YEARS AGO	135 MILLION YEARS AGO

65 MILLION YEARS AGO

MANIRAPTOR OR NOT?

The true maniraptors are the dromaeosaurs, oviraptorosaurs, troodontids (big-eyed brainy meat-eaters), avialans, and modern birds. Yet there are other groups of coelurosaurs which may also be maniraptors. The bizarre, big-clawed therizinosaurs, such as *Erlikosaurus*, have similar hands to those of dromaeosaurs and oviraptorosaurs. Ornithomimosaurs and tyrannosaurs lack the special maniraptor wrist, but their ancestors probably had it. Together, true maniraptors, therizinosaurs, ornithomimosaurs, and tyrannosaurs form the group maniraptoriformes.

Hands that fly
Dromaeosaurs, oviraptorosaurs, and modern birds all have similar forelimbs. Their wrist bones and elbow joints allowed dromaeosaurs and oviraptorosaurs to fold their hands out of the way against their bodies as they ran. The same features let them shoot their arms forward to grab prey. These wrists and elbows also enabled birds to fly. They allowed them to beat their wings, driving them through the air.

How did (and do) they live?
Dromaeosaurs and troodontids were smart predators. Oviraptorosaurs were toothless

and may have eaten both meat and plants. Birds are the most varied group of all.

Modern birds range from tiny hummingbirds to the fast-running ostrich. In part, birds have survived because they could fly. Their wings would not work as they do today if they had not evolved from a maniraptor wrist.

CHECK THESE OUT!

Archaeopteryx, Avialans, Birds, Dromaeosaurs, *Erlikosaurus*, *Oviraptor*, Oviraptorosaurs, Saurischian dinosaurs, *Struthiomimus*, Theropods, *Troodon*, Tyrannosaurs, *Utahraptor*, *Velociraptor*

Massospondylus

Richard Owen, the British scientist who invented the word *dinosaur*, named *Massospondylus* in 1854. He had only a single tail bone to study. Today paleontologists have many *Massospondylus* skeletons.

Massospondylus belonged to a group of long-necked dinosaurs called the prosauropods. They were ancestors of the sauropods, the big, long-necked, long-tailed plant-eaters like *Apatosaurus*.

Massospondylus was a fairly large prosauropod, although smaller than *Lufengosaurus* and *Plateosaurus*. It was common in southern Africa at the beginning of the Jurassic period.

SEE HOW THEY GROW

Most dinosaurs are known from only a handful of specimens. In these cases, it is often impossible to tell the difference between males and females or to see how the dinosaurs grew. However, collectors have found many specimens of *Massospondylus*, so paleontologists are able to study how it grew. Fossil-hunters have found some very small specimens of *Massospondylus*. These were probably juveniles. Juveniles had big eyes and few teeth. Larger specimens show us that as *Massospondylus* grew, the head caught up with the eyes and more teeth grew in. Some paleontologists think they can tell the difference between male and female *Massospondylus*. They think males had stronger skulls, with thickened bones above their eyes and in their upper jaws.

◀ Besides reaching high into trees, *Massospondylus*'s long neck would have helped the dinosaur to feed over a wide area of ground while standing still.

How did it live?

Like all prosauropods, *Massospondylus* ate plants. However, it lived in fairly dry areas with little vegetation. Some paleontologists believe it may have eaten small animals from time to time when it was short of plant food.

Footprints indicate that most prosauropods usually walked on all fours. *Massospondylus*'s hind legs were bigger than its forelegs, so it probably walked on two legs, too. This ability let *Massospondylus* reach higher into the trees for food.

Like other prosauropods, *Massospondylus* had a large claw on each thumb. It may have used these claws to dig for food and water or to defend against meat–eating dinosaurs.

A transatlantic dinosaur?

Besides southern Africa, *Massospondylus* remains have also been discovered in Arizona. How did it cross the Atlantic Ocean? It did not need to. In the Early Jurassic period, the earth's continents were much closer together than they are today. The Atlantic had only just begun to open, and northwest Africa and eastern North America were still joined. Dinosaurs could cross on dry land between the two continents.

CHECK THESE OUT!

Apatosaurus, Collecting dinosaurs, Continental drift, Jurassic period, *Lufengosaurus*, *Plateosaurus*, Prosauropods, Saurischian dinosaurs, Sauropods

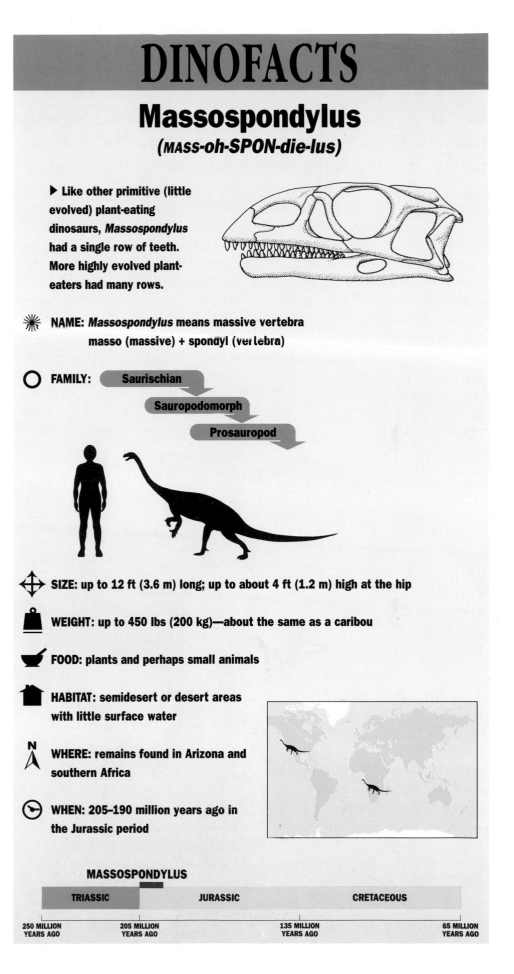

DINOFACTS

Massospondylus
(MASS-oh-SPON-die-lus)

▶ Like other primitive (little evolved) plant-eating dinosaurs, *Massospondylus* had a single row of teeth. More highly evolved plant-eaters had many rows.

NAME: *Massospondylus* means massive vertebra
masso (massive) + spondyl (vertebra)

FAMILY: Saurischian → Sauropodomorph → Prosauropod

SIZE: up to 12 ft (3.6 m) long; up to about 4 ft (1.2 m) high at the hip

WEIGHT: up to 450 lbs (200 kg)—about the same as a caribou

FOOD: plants and perhaps small animals

HABITAT: semidesert or desert areas with little surface water

WHERE: remains found in Arizona and southern Africa

WHEN: 205–190 million years ago in the Jurassic period

MASSOSPONDYLUS

TRIASSIC	JURASSIC	CRETACEOUS
250 MILLION YEARS AGO	205 MILLION YEARS AGO	135 MILLION YEARS AGO	65 MILLION YEARS AGO

Megalosaurus

Megalosaurus was the first dinosaur ever described. The scientists who first studied it knew almost nothing about dinosaurs, and even today, paleontologists scratch their heads over this puzzling find.

In 1677, Englishman Robert Plot wrote a nature book. In it he described a fossil bone, found in England, which he believed came from an ancient giant human. Scientists are now fairly sure that the fossil that Plot described was the end of a leg bone from the dinosaur *Megalosaurus*.

leg bones. English scientist William Buckland first described *Megalosaurus* from these newly discovered bones in 1824, although it was another English scientist, James Parkinson, who made up the dinosaur's name, *Megalosaurus*, which means "the great lizard," two years before that in 1822.

Mission impossible
Even though *Megalosaurus* was the first dinosaur known to science, it is by no means the best known. Scientists know that it walked on two legs and ate meat, but they are unsure about almost everything else.

Buckland did not have enough good quality bones to

First-known dinosaur
In the early 19th century, *Megalosaurus* became the first dinosaur known to science. In 1818, some more giant bones were discovered in an English quarry. They included a lower jaw with large, jagged-edged teeth, some backbones, the right shoulder, an arm bone, parts of the hips, and several

▲ Scientists know little for certain about *Megalosaurus*, except that it was a large meat-eating dinosaur that moved on its long, strong hind legs.

▶ Because *Megalosaurus* was so poorly known, scientists gave its name to many similar-looking fossils. One such fossil is now called *Eustreptospondylus*.

make an accurate description. Also, the science of identifying and describing animals and plants was then still fairly new.

Today when scientists study a new set of dinosaur bones, they can compare them to bones of already-known dinosaurs. In 1824, though, the *Megalosaurus* bones were all that scientists had to begin describing a totally new group of animals. Buckland and others had a tough time, because they had nothing with which to compare *Megalosaurus*.

Eustreptospondylus oxoniensis

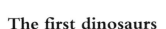

The first dinosaurs
Megalosaurus was an extremely important find. It was soon followed by two other English discoveries, *Iguanodon* and *Hylaeosaurus*. The 19th-century scientists who studied these animals' remains realized their bones were different from any they had seen before. However, they did not call them dinosaurs at first. It was English scientist Richard Owen who first called them dinosaurs. He saw that the bones of these three large animals shared some features. In 1842, he placed them in a new group of animals—the dinosaurs, or terrible lizards.

Megalosaurus, *Iguanodon*, and *Hylaeosaurus* became the first dinosaurs. When Owen called them terrible, he meant dinosaurs were frighteningly big. At that time no one knew how many types of dinosaurs there were.

Strange relations
Since *Megalosaurus* was first described more than 150 years ago, there have been as many as 26 more *Megalosaurus* finds reported. If these fossils are all *Megalosaurus*, then it lived all over the world.

THE LANGUAGE OF SCIENCE

To be recognized scientifically, an animal or plant has to have its description and name published in a scientific journal. Scientists write articles in scientific journals for other scientists. They use complicated scientific language. By using technical words and phrases in journal articles, scientists can communicate quickly with each other. A few big words are equal to many sentences, or even paragraphs, of everyday speech. Scientific language also lets scientists describe their ideas and results as accurately as possible. Different branches of science, like paleontology or astronomy (the study of stars and planets), each have their own sets of words and ideas that every paleontologist or astronomer knows about. Everyone reading complicated technical words in journals also agrees on what those words mean too.

Publishing the name of a newfound animal or plant, and showing drawings or photographs of it (or its remains), lets the whole world learn about a new discovery. When possible, scientists name an animal using the most complete specimen. Sometimes they cannot get a complete animal or plant. For example, dinosaurs are identified from their bones. Even today, some sea animals are known only from parts of their bodies—the largest giant squid is known only from pieces of giant tentacle.

dinosaur *Eustreptospondylus*, which means "well-curved backbone."

An American brother?

Mysterious *Megalosaurus* may have lived in North America. Some paleontologists believe *Torvosaurus* may be a kind of *Megalosaurus*. *Torvosaurus* was found in Late Jurassic rocks in Colorado and Wyoming. It is known only from a few bits and pieces of bone and skull.

However, so far all definite *Megalosaurus* remains come from Europe. So does that mean *Torvosaurus* cannot be a kind of *Megalosaurus* because it lived in North America? No. During much of the Mesozoic Era, the earth's continents were in different positions from those of today. During the Jurassic period, the Atlantic Ocean was only just beginning to form. Western Europe and North America were joined together in a single landmass.

A French cousin?

Another dinosaur very similar to *Megalosaurus* lived in Europe during the Jurassic period. Called *Poekilopleuron*, it lived in France and may have been a close relative of *Megalosaurus* and *Torvosaurus*.

Today a seaway called the English Channel separates England and France. However, just as North America and Western Europe were joined in the Jurassic, so were England and France. The English Channel did not exist. Dinosaurs could wander to and fro between England and the rest of Europe.

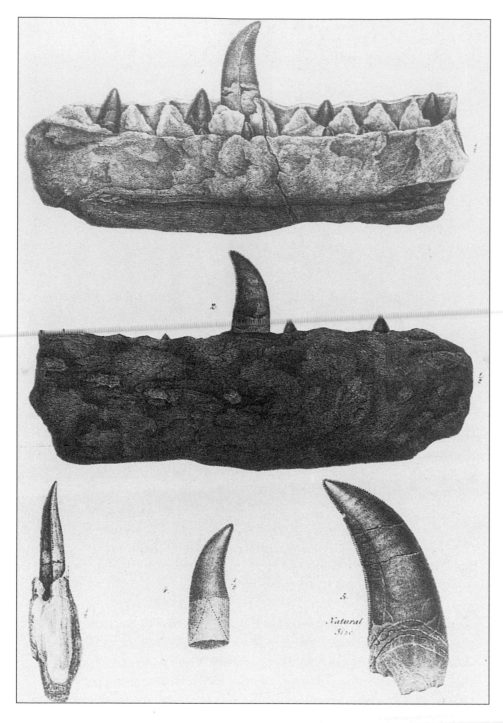

▲ The right lower jaw and teeth of meat-eating *Megalosaurus*. The daggerlike teeth have jagged edges that could have ripped through a victim's skin, muscle, and bone.

However, paleontologists are not sure if these fossils are all *Megalosaurus*. They may belong to other meat-eating dinosaurs.

For example, in the 19th century, fossil-hunters found the remains of a large theropod (two-legged meat-eater). Early paleontologists thought it was another *Megalosaurus*. Scientists accepted this description for more than 100 years. In 1964, however, English scientist Alick Walker showed that this dinosaur was different from Buckland's *Megalosaurus*. Walker named the new

Unfortunately, the bones of *Poekilopleuron* were destroyed during World War II. We will have to wait for new finds to see if *Poekilopleuron* really was a close relative of *Megalosaurus*.

How *Megalosaurus* lived

Like most meat-eating dinosaurs, *Megalosaurus* would probably have killed and eaten other large dinosaurs. We would have to find a skeleton that clearly held the remains of its last meal to be sure.

Like the later tyrannosaurs, to which it was not closely related, *Megalosaurus* had short arms. These would have been useless for grabbing prey, although the dinosaur may have been able to pick at remains from other dinosaurs' kills. Like the tyrannosaurs, *Megalosaurus* also had a big head and long teeth. Its head contained large, powerful muscles to work the jaws.

Scientists have worked out how the jaw muscles were arranged in the skull. They can tell that *Megalosaurus* was able to snap its jaws shut very quickly to bite prey. Like a crocodile's, its bite would have been deadly. The jaws of a large modern crocodile can bite an antelope clean in two! *Megalosaurus*'s could have crunched through thick dinosaur bones.

Megalosaurus's teeth had jagged edges (serrations), a bit like the blades of a saw. These serrations would have helped the teeth to slice through a plant-eater's skin and muscles. *Megalosaurus* did not chew its food; it had no cheeks with

which to chew. If *Megalosaurus* had tried to chew, the meat would have spilled out of the sides of its mouth. Instead, the dinosaur sheared off bite-sized chunks from its prey and swallowed them whole.

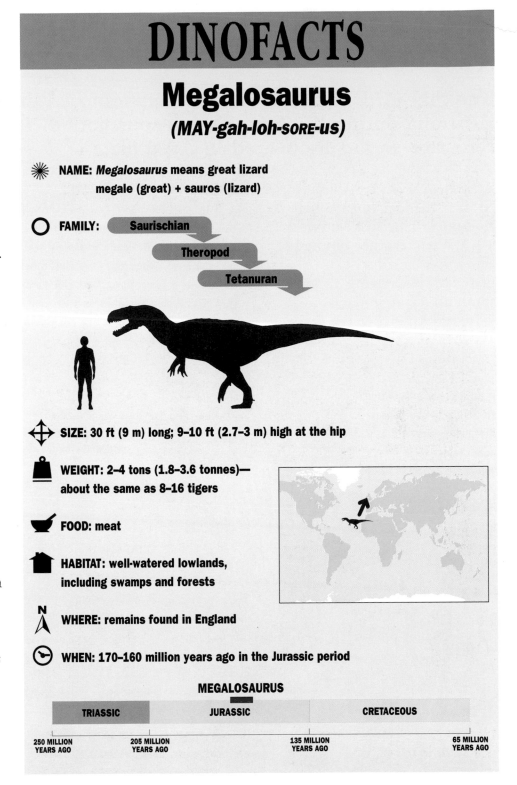

DINOFACTS

Megalosaurus
(MAY-gah-loh-SORE-us)

✳ **NAME:** *Megalosaurus* means great lizard
megale (great) + sauros (lizard)

◯ **FAMILY:** Saurischian → Theropod → Tetanuran

✛ **SIZE:** 30 ft (9 m) long; 9–10 ft (2.7–3 m) high at the hip

WEIGHT: 2–4 tons (1.8–3.6 tonnes)—about the same as 8–16 tigers

FOOD: meat

HABITAT: well-watered lowlands, including swamps and forests

WHERE: remains found in England

WHEN: 170–160 million years ago in the Jurassic period

MEGALOSAURUS

	TRIASSIC	JURASSIC	CRETACEOUS
250 MILLION YEARS AGO	205 MILLION YEARS AGO	135 MILLION YEARS AGO	65 MILLION YEARS AGO

CHECK THESE OUT!

Bones, Collecting dinosaurs, Continental drift, Dinosaurs, *Iguanodon*, Jurassic period, Saurischian dinosaurs, Tetanurans, Theropods, Tyrannosaurs

Minmi

Tanklike *Minmi* was an ankylosaur (armored dinosaur) that lived in Australia during the Early Cretaceous period. It is the most complete dinosaur so far discovered in Australia.

Australian scientist Ralph Molnar named *Minmi* after studying a partial skeleton in 1977. Unlike other dinosaurs, this ankylosaur had extra platelike bones lying along its spine under its skin.

In 1989, rancher Ian Ievers discovered a second *Minmi* specimen. This skeleton was in

SINK OR FLOAT

Both *Minmi* specimens fossilized in silt and mud at the bottom of the ocean. How did they get there? There are two likely explanations, but either way the dinosaurs died on land. First, *Minmi* may have died, dried out, and then been washed into the sea. Eventually it would have filled with water and sunk. Second, *Minmi* washed out to sea just after it died. Gases in its body would have kept it afloat. In the end, though, the carcass would have burst. The gas would have been released and the body would have sunk to the bottom.

▶ *Minmi* was a low-slung, slow-moving plant-eater that lived along rivers near the coast. It was more lightly armored than most of its ankylosaur cousins.

better condition than the first. It was missing only its feet and the last two thirds of its tail. Molnar studied the new specimen. It was about the same size as the first and had the same unusual backbones. Molnar now thinks it may be a new kind of *Minmi*.

Australian tank

Minmi had a broad, low skull with a short, pointed snout. Like all ankylosaurs, *Minmi* had a wide body.

Minmi had 20 rows of small armor plates, or scutes, running from its neck to its hips. Bony triangular plates ran down the sides of its tail. These plates could have hurt an attacking meat-eater if *Minmi* had lashed out with its tail.

Early model

Minmi seems to have been a primitive (little evolved) ankylosaur. *Minmi*'s ancestors may have been stranded in the world's southern landmasses when Pangaea broke up in the Jurassic period. Far from other ankylosaurs, these *Minmi* ancestors would have evolved in different ways.

CHECK THESE OUT!

Ankylosaurs, *Ankylosaurus*, Continental drift, Cretaceous period, Jurassic period, Ornithischian dinosaurs, Thyreophorans

DINOFACTS

Minmi
(MIN-mee)

✳ **NAME:** *Minmi* is named in honor of the Minmi Crossing, Australia, where it was first found

⭕ **FAMILY:** Ornithischian → Thyreophoran → Ankylosaur

✛ **SIZE:** 9–10 ft (2.7–3 m) long; 4 ft (1.2 m) high at the hip

⚖ **WEIGHT:** 400–600 lbs (180–270 kg)—about the same as a brown bear

🍵 **FOOD:** low-growing vegetation

🏠 **HABITAT:** coastal lowland

🧭 **WHERE:** remains found in Australia

🕐 **WHEN:** 115–105 million years ago in the Cretaceous period

			MINMI	
TRIASSIC		JURASSIC		CRETACEOUS
250 MILLION YEARS AGO	205 MILLION YEARS AGO		135 MILLION YEARS AGO	65 MILLION YEARS AGO

Mononykus

This Late Cretaceous dinosaur has got scientists puzzled. It probably ran fast, and may have been an early bird, but how did it use its tiny arms and single-clawed hands?

In 1987, a joint Soviet and Mongolian fossil-hunting expedition found a small skeleton in Mongolia's Gobi Desert. The skeleton lay in Late Cretaceous rocks. The paleontologists found the back of the animal's head, most of its backbone, its forelimbs, its hind legs, its shoulders, and portions of its hips. From its long, strong hind legs, they could see the dinosaur was a two-legged walker.

In 1992, Malcolm McKenna, an expert on mammals at the American Museum of Natural

▼ **Mononykus had short, thick arms. Its long legs would have helped it to run at speed. How Mononykus used its arms is still a mystery.**

History (AMNH), found part of a smaller dinosaur skeleton in Mongolia. It lay in older rocks but may be the same kind of dinosaur as the larger, 1987 find.

Single claw

Mongolian paleontologist Perle Altangerel, along with Mark Norell, Luis Chiappe, and Jim Clark of the AMNH, described these two skeletons in 1993. These scientists reckoned both belonged to the same kind of dinosaur. They named it *Mononykus* (single claw), because it had only one claw on each hand.

Mononykus had a long neck and tail, long, slender legs, and a small head. Its upper jaw was

mostly toothless. Although *Mononykus* was birdlike it clearly could not fly. Its thick, stumpy arms were too short to work as wings.

Scientists think *Mononykus* was more closely related to modern birds than was *Archaeopteryx*, the earliest-known of the avialans (the group including birds and their closest relatives). Like modern birds, *Mononykus* had a long, ridged breastbone. The bone supports birds' powerful flight muscles. *Mononykus* had other birdlike features, too. Its lower leg bones narrowed to thin points near its ankles. Part of the upper pelvic bone in its hips was very wide. The way *Mononykus*'s thigh muscles were attached to its leg bones was also birdlike. The scientists who described *Mononykus* decided it was a primitive (little evolved), flightless early bird.

Early bird, or not?

Not all scientists agree that *Mononykus* was an early bird. Yale University's John Ostrom is a pioneer in bird–dinosaur relationships and an expert on *Archaeopteryx* and the dromaeosaur (clawed

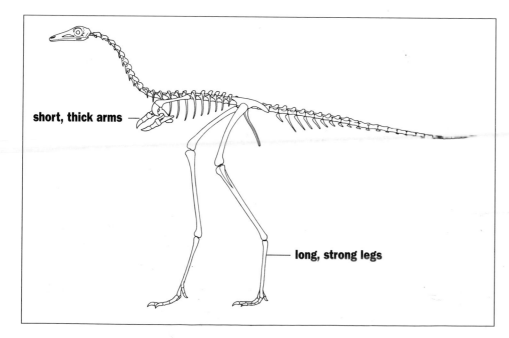

short, thick arms

long, strong legs

hunter) *Deinonychus*. He does not think that *Mononykus* was an early bird. He believes instead that it evolved birdlike features separately from birds.

Ostrom thinks *Mononykus*'s breastbone became enlarged as the animal's arms got thicker and stronger. He believes that the birdlike features in the hips and legs evolved to help

▼ The earliest birds had teeth and long tails. Even if *Mononykus* really could not fly, it probably would have had feathers.

Mononykus to run fast. Some other fossil bird experts agree with Ostrom.

In 1994, fossil-hunters found a *Mononykus* specimen with a complete skull. Although paleontologists have not yet described it, researchers at the AMNH have seen some more birdlike features in this skull.

What was *Mononykus*?
Based on how animals are described and grouped today, all dinosaurs can be traced back to a common ancestor. All dinosaurs, whether saurischian (lizard-hipped) or ornithischian (bird-hipped), descended from this common ancestor. Most scientists now agree that birds descended from theropod (two-legged meat-eating) dinosaurs. This means all birds are theropod dinosaurs, but not all theropods are birds.

Scientists used to place all birds in the group called Aves, with *Archaeopteryx* as the first bird. Today, however, only modern birds are Aves. Modern birds have a short tail and no teeth. The Aves group now includes the common ancestor of all modern bird groups and all its descendants. *Archaeopteryx* and all of its early bird descendants are avialans.

BEATEN BY A BEETLE

Mononykus was first described as *Mononychus*. Later the paleontologists learned that the name *Mononychus* had already been used for a beetle. With animal names, it is first come, first served. Because the beetle was named first, it kept the name *Mononychus*. In a second paper, the paleontologists renamed their dinosaur *Mononykus*. Considering that several million kinds of animals have lived on earth, it is easy to see why naming all those animals gets so complicated.

The avialan group includes both early and modern birds. Therefore all birds are avialans, but not all avialans are modern birds. So what was *Mononykus*? It was a theropod dinosaur. It was probably an avialan, too. However, either way, toothy, long-tailed *Mononykus* was not a modern bird.

Unusual arms
Although many theropods have evolved shorter arms, it is very rare to see theropod arms get shorter *and* thicker. *Mononykus* had short, thick arms. Its arm bones had big fixing points to hold its powerful muscles.

Mononykus's palm bones were joined into one short, solid bone. Its strong, well-developed thumb had a large

claw. *Mononykus* means single claw, but there are places on its hand where there may have been two more tiny fingers.

Burrowing bird?
Almost all paleontologists agree that *Mononykus*'s arms were shaped like the arms of burrowing animals like moles. The large muscle attachments, efficient joints, and thick bones suggest a powerful digging arm. However, scientists cannot imagine a burrowing animal shaped like *Mononykus*. Standing on its long legs, it could not easily have reached the ground with its short arms!

Some scientists think that *Mononykus* may have used its claws to rip open termite mounds, just as giant anteaters do today in South America.

▲ Anteaters use their long, thick, sharp claws to tear open anthills and termite nests in order to eat the insects. Perhaps *Mononykus* did the same.

Termites are small insects that live together in huge colonies. The termite colonies build mounds and towers of dirt. Baked in the sun, the dirt becomes as hard as stone. It is not easy to open a termite mound unless you have very thick, sharp claws.

The first *Mononykus*
Following the 1987 discovery of *Mononykus*, paleontologists realized they had had a *Mononykus* specimen all along! In 1923, a party led by American fossil-hunter Roy Chapman Andrews had collected several bones at the

Flaming Cliffs in Mongolia. Amid their collection of mammals, dinosaur eggs, small theropods, and the small ceratopsian (horned dinosaur) *Protoceratops*, were the pelvis and leg of *Mononykus*. However, no one knew about *Mononykus* in 1923, so Andrews had labeled it simply a birdlike dinosaur.

Mononykus relatives

Argentine paleontologist Fernando Novas found close relatives of *Mononykus* in Cretaceous rocks in Argentina, South America. How did these early birds get from Asia to South America?

In the Mesozoic Era, the earth's landmasses were not in the same positions as they are today. Sea levels changed, and at times, land bridges linked areas that are now separated by ocean. Dinosaurs could move from one continent to another. Scientists believe *Mononykus*-like dinosaurs probably lived in Europe and Africa, as well as in Asia and South America.

How *Mononykus* lived

Mononykus had long, strong legs, so it could have run fast over the desert sand dunes and wooded plains of Mongolia. It probably ate insects and small lizards and mammals.

CHECK THESE OUT!

Archaeopteryx, Avialans, Birds, Continental drift, Cretaceous period, Deinonychus, Eggs and babies, Evolution, Protoceratops, Saurischian dinosaurs, Theropods

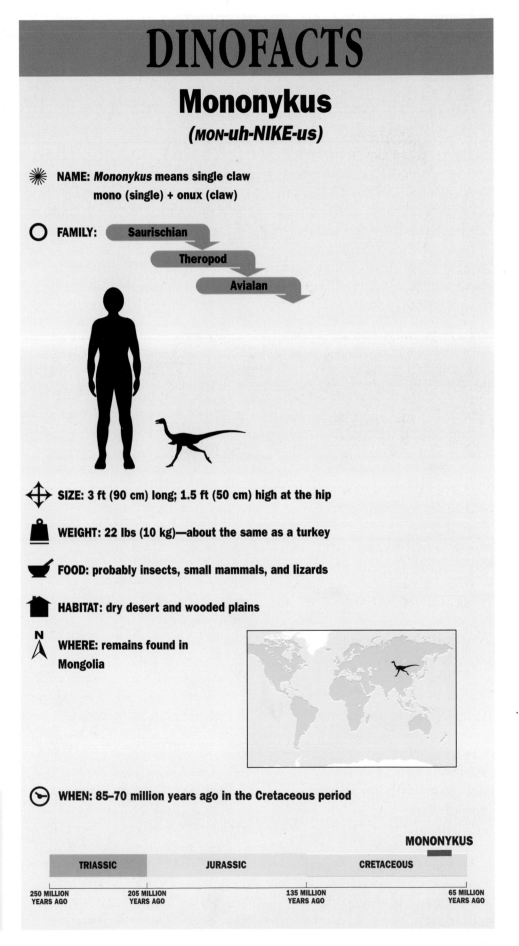

DINOFACTS

Mononykus
(MON-uh-NIKE-us)

NAME: *Mononykus* means single claw
mono (single) + onux (claw)

FAMILY: Saurischian → Theropod → Avialan

SIZE: 3 ft (90 cm) long; 1.5 ft (50 cm) high at the hip

WEIGHT: 22 lbs (10 kg)—about the same as a turkey

FOOD: probably insects, small mammals, and lizards

HABITAT: dry desert and wooded plains

WHERE: remains found in Mongolia

WHEN: 85–70 million years ago in the Cretaceous period

TRIASSIC	JURASSIC	CRETACEOUS	MONONYKUS
250 MILLION YEARS AGO	205 MILLION YEARS AGO	135 MILLION YEARS AGO	65 MILLION YEARS AGO

Mosasaurs

Mosasaurs were not dinosaurs, but they hunted the other animals that shared the coastal waters of the warm Late Cretaceous seas. Some kinds reached 30 ft (9 m), longer than a great white shark!

During most of the Cretaceous period the oceans were much higher than they are today. The sea flooded large areas of what is now dry land. It was in these warm, shallow seas that the mosasaurs swam.

Mosasaurs were reptiles, but not dinosaurs. Their ancestors were probably big land lizards related to modern animals like the 10 ft (3 m) Komodo dragon of Asia. Mosasaurs' cousins were the snakes.

Over millions of years, mosasaurs slowly evolved into better swimmers and hunters.

▼ Mosasaurs in action. A huge, fanged *Tylosaurus* swoops between *Clidastes* (top) and *Platecarpus* (bottom).

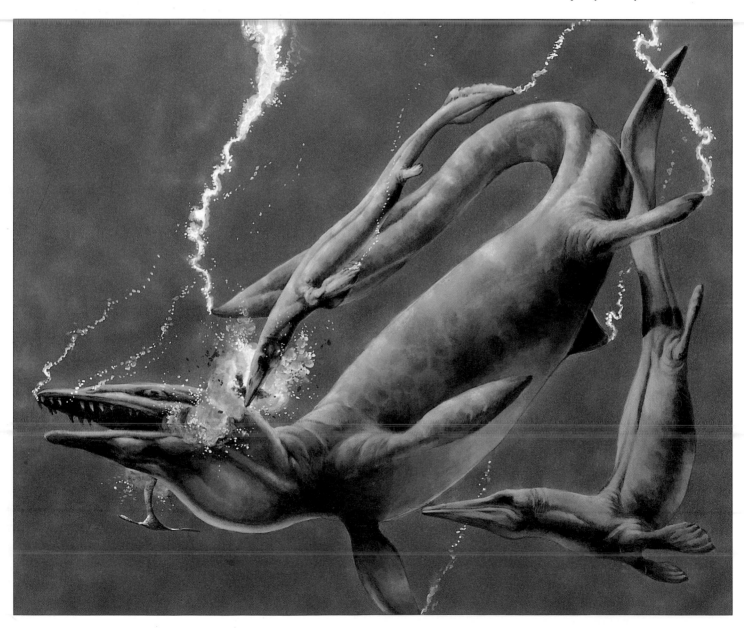

Their bodies became long and eel-like. Like eels, they swam by swinging their bodies from side to side. Their arms and legs evolved into paddles, and their fingers and toes became covered by mittens of muscle.

How did mosasaurs live?

Mosasaurs ate fish and squid-like animals called ammonoids. Collectors have found large ammonoid shells scarred with the V-shaped teeth marks that a mosasaur would make.

Because they were firmly set in deep sockets, like those of the meat-eating dinosaurs, mosasaurs' teeth were much stronger than those of their lizard ancestors. Mosasaurs shared the seas with other fierce hunters, the ichthyosaurs and the plesiosaurs.

CHECK THESE OUT!

Ammonoids; Coral reefs; Cretaceous period; Dinosaurs; Evolution; Extinction; Fish; Ichthyosaurs; Lizards and snakes; Plesiosaurs, pliosaurs, and nothosaurs; Reptiles

FOSSIL FACTS

Mosasaurs
(MOH-zuh-sores)

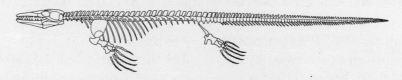

▲ Collectors have found hundreds of mosasaur skeletons all over the world. *Platecarpus*—14 ft (4.3 m) long—lived in Belgium and the United States.

✳ **NAME:** Mosasaur means lizard from the Meuse
Mosa (form of the name of the Meuse River in Belgium) + sauros (lizard)

◯ **FAMILY:** Reptile

✛ **SIZE:** up to 30 ft (9 m) long

FOOD: fish, small marine reptiles, ammonoids, belemnoids, shellfish

HABITAT: warm, shallow, coastal seas

WHERE: remains found in Belgium, Canada, Netherlands, New Zealand, North Africa, and the United States

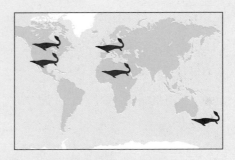

WHEN: 75—65 million years ago in the Cretaceous period

			MOSASAURS
TRIASSIC	JURASSIC	CRETACEOUS	
250 MILLION YEARS AGO	205 MILLION YEARS AGO	135 MILLION YEARS AGO	65 MILLION YEARS AGO

Mussaurus

Mussaurus was a fairly early dinosaur. Paleontologists have only found the bones of young *Mussaurus*, but they think it was an ancestor of the sauropods, the big, long-necked plant-eaters.

In the late 1970s, Argentine paleontologists José Bonaparte and Martin Vince found a very small dinosaur skeleton in Late Triassic rocks in Patagonia, southern Argentina. They also discovered enough bones to assemble nine more skeletons.

Because they were so small and found so close together, Bonaparte and Vince thought the fossils belonged to baby dinosaurs that had died close to their nest.

Mouse lizard
The new dinosaur's skeleton fits comfortably in the palm of a man's hand. Bonaparte and Vince named the animal *Mussaurus*, or mouse lizard.

The tiny bones of very young dinosaurs are difficult to find and identify. They blend in with the dirt. Also, they have not yet formed all the special features that help paleontologists to tell to which kind of dinosaur they belong.

CUTE LIZARD

Mussaurus is one of the few dinosaurs for which scientists have a complete juvenile skeleton. Like a human baby, *Mussaurus* had a big head and a short neck. It had a short nose and big, round eyes. Biologists believe babies evolved to look cute so their mothers will always take care of them, however annoying their crying and messes might be. Perhaps baby dinosaurs were cute for the same reason.

▼ A *Mussaurus* stands next to the egg from which it has just hatched. This tiny, wide-eyed creature looks like a dinosaur but was only about the size of a puppy!

Mussaurus's skull had a short snout like that of a sauropod. Sauropods were long-necked, long-tailed, plant-eating dinosaurs like *Apatosaurus*, *Brachiosaurus*, and *Camarasaurus*.

However, the rest of *Mussaurus*'s skeleton from its neck to the tip of its tail was very similar to that of a prosauropod. Prosauropods, such as *Lufengosaurus* and *Massospondylus*, lived from the Late Triassic period to the Early Jurassic period. They were the ancestors of the sauropods (*prosauropod* means "before sauropods").

Like the sauropods, the prosauropods had long necks and tails and ate plants. However, while sauropods walked on all fours, some kinds of prosauropods could walk on just their hind legs.

Is *Mussaurus* a prosauropod? Paleontologists think so. They have a set of prosauropod skeletons from hatchling to adult which show how prosauropods grew. This set shows that *Mussaurus* could have grown up to be a prosauropod like the sturdy, Late Triassic *Plateosaurus*.

Because no one knows for sure what an adult *Mussaurus* was like, scientists can only guess how this animal lived. If *Mussaurus* was a prosauropod, we can assume it ate plants.

CHECK THESE OUT!

Eggs and babies, *Lufengosaurus*, *Massospondylus*, Plants, *Plateosaurus*, Prosauropods, Saurischian dinosaurs, Sauropods, Triassic period

DINOFACTS

Mussaurus
(muh-SORE-us)

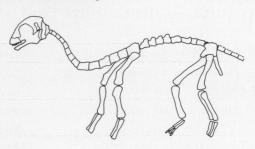

▶ **Mussaurus** is known only from its young. If someone finds a fully grown mouse lizard, perhaps its name will need to be changed.

✳ **NAME:** *Mussaurus* means mouse lizard
    mus (mouse) + sauros (lizard)

○ **FAMILY:** Saurischian → Sauropodomorph → Prosauropod

✛ **SIZE:** (as a baby) 16 in (40 cm) long; 2.2 in (5.7 cm) high at the hip

WEIGHT: 3.5–14 oz (100–400 g)—about the same as 1–2 ground squirrels

FOOD: plants

HABITAT: unknown

WHERE: remains found in Argentina

WHEN: 215 million years ago in the Triassic period

MUSSAURUS		
TRIASSIC	JURASSIC	CRETACEOUS
250 MILLION YEARS AGO	205 MILLION YEARS AGO	135 MILLION YEARS AGO · 65 MILLION YEARS AGO

Muttaburrasaurus

In 1981, a new plant-eating dinosaur was named: *Muttaburrasaurus*. This animal is especially interesting because it was discovered in Australia, a continent that has not yet produced many dinosaurs.

That *Muttaburrasaurus* comes from Australia is important for two reasons. The first reason is that dinosaurs are only rarely discovered in Australia. The second reason is that *Muttaburrasaurus* is an iguanodontid, one of the plant-eating dinosaurs with spiky thumbs named after *Iguanodon*. Iguanodontids have been found in Early Cretaceous rocks in Africa, Asia, Europe, and North America. Finding one in Australia shows how widespread this group of dinosaurs became.

Bird-hipped dinosaurs

The iguanodontids belonged to a larger group called ornithischian, or bird-hipped, dinosaurs. Most ornithischians had a pubis (the front bone of the lower hip) that pointed backward. Their lower jaw had an extra bone that is absent from the jaws of saurischian (lizard-hipped) dinosaurs, the other main dinosaur group.

▶ **Muttaburrasaurus had a hollow bump on its snout. Scientists do not know what this bump was used for. Perhaps the dinosaur could blow through this bump to make sounds. Perhaps the bump just gave the dinosaur a great sense of smell.**

EMPTY DESERTS

Australia is a large continent and is mostly desert. Dry, treeless desert areas are usually good places to look for fossils. That way, nothing (not buildings, not trees, not even soil) will hide them. The large areas of desert in Australia have not produced many dinosaur fossils, though. Why is this?

First, northern lands, like Europe and North America, have freezing cold winters. Many years of freezing and thawing cause rocks to splinter and crack, exposing fossils. The climate of Australia, however, does not produce severe winter weather.

Second, it seems that the Australian climate has been dry for many thousands of years. For fossils to be exposed at the earth's surface, the top layer of rocks has to be worn down by wind and rain. Streams and rivers need to flow for many years to cut into cliffs and mountains. Only when the rocky areas are worn down and cleared of sands and gravels can people see parts of skeletons poking out of the ground.

Odd one out

Muttaburrasaurus was an unusual iguanodontid, though. A special feature of the iguanodontids was their jaw. Before the iguanodontids, dinosaur jaws opened and closed like scissors. Most iguanodontids' jaws were different than this. Their lower jaw still moved up and down, but their upper jaw could move from side to side. This movement allowed their teeth to rub past each other to grind food thoroughly.

Muttaburrasaurus's upper jaws could not make sideways movements. Its jaws worked like scissors, as did those of meat-eating dinosaurs and early plant-eaters. However, paleontologists still think it was an iguanodontid. Like others in that group, it had a large skull for its body size and big, bony thumb spikes on its hands.

How did it live?

Like other iguanodontids, *Muttaburrasaurus* ate plants. Like all advanced (highly evolved) ornithischians, it had muscular cheeks, which allowed it to chew leaves and stems. Less evolved plant-eaters had less well developed cheeks and had to swallow their food whole or almost whole.

Besides this, scientists know little of *Muttaburrasaurus*'s lifestyle. They need more of its fossils. However, dinosaur remains are so rare in Australia, that it may be many years before we know more about mysterious *Muttaburrasaurus*.

CHECK THESE OUT!

Cretaceous period, Dinosaurs, *Iguanodon*, Ornithischian dinosaurs, Ornithopods, Saurischian dinosaurs

DINOFACTS

Muttaburrasaurus

(MUH-*tah*-BUH-*rah*-SORE-*us*)

NAME: *Muttaburrasaurus* means Muttaburra lizard
Muttaburra (town in Australia) + sauros (lizard)

FAMILY: Ornithischian
Ornithopod

WEIGHT: 4 tons (3.6 tonnes)—about the same as 4 North American bison.

FOOD: plants

HABITAT: well-watered lowlands

WHERE: remains found in Australia

SIZE: 23 ft (7 m) long; 10 ft (3 m) high at the hip

WHEN: 120 million years ago in the Cretaceous period

MUTTABURRASAURUS

TRIASSIC	JURASSIC	CRETACEOUS
250 MILLION YEARS AGO	205 MILLION YEARS AGO	135 MILLION YEARS AGO / 65 MILLION YEARS AGO

Nanotyrannus

Known only from a fossil skull, *Nanotyrannus* is now thought by many paleontologists to be a juvenile (young) *Tyrannosaurus*. However, it just might be a tiny cousin of the king of predators.

In 1942, a team from the Cleveland Museum of Natural History discovered the skull of a tyrannosaur in Montana. The skull was just 22 in (57 cm)—small for a tyrannosaur.

Smithsonian Institution paleontologist Charles Gilmore thought the skull might have belonged to a young tyrannosaur like *Tyrannosaurus*. In the end, though, Gilmore decided it was an adult of a new kind of *Gorgosaurus*, another tyrannosaur. One of the main reasons he thought it was an adult was that some of the skull bones were fused together, as they were in most adult dinosaurs.

The little tyrant
In the mid-1980s, US paleontologists Robert Bakker, Philip Currie, and Michael Williams reexamined the skull. Because of the fused bones, they agreed that it was an adult tyrannosaur's skull, but not a *Gorgosaurus*'s. The skull is much wider at the back than at the front. The only tyrannosaur with a skull that shape was *Tyrannosaurus*. The skull is too small for an adult

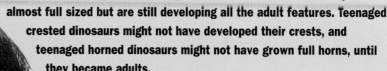

FROM EGG TO ADULT
Like other animals, dinosaurs passed through a number of stages on their way to becoming adults. Most paleontologists recognize four main growth stages—embryo, juvenile, subadult, and adult. Embryos are unhatched babies still in their eggs. Juveniles include all dinosaurs from hatchlings (ones that just broke out of their eggs) to those that are close to being fully grown. Just before adulthood, dinosaurs become subadults. Subadults are the "teenagers" of the dinosaur world. They are almost full sized but are still developing all the adult features. Teenaged crested dinosaurs might not have developed their crests, and teenaged horned dinosaurs might not have grown full horns, until they became adults.

Tyrannosaurus, so it must belong to a new tyrannosaur. The team named the dinosaur *Nanotyrannus*, the dwarf tyrant.

Not all paleontologists agree that *Nanotyrannus* was a small but adult tyrannosaur. Most believe it was a juvenile *Tyrannosaurus*. Paleontologists need to find good remains of an adult and juvenile *Tyrannosaurus* together. They could then compare the young dinosaur's skull with *Nanotyrannus*'s.

However, one day paleontologists may find the remains of a large *Nanotyrannus* and discover that the dinosaur they already have is just a juvenile *Nanotyrannus*.

◀ Was *Nanotyrannus* a young *Tyrannosaurus* or the smallest of the tyrannosaurs? Scientists need more information before they can say for sure.

CHECK THESE OUT!

Cretaceous period, Saurischian dinosaurs, Tetanurans, Theropods, Tyrannosaurs, *Tyrannosaurus*

DINOFACTS

Nanotyrannus
(NAN-oh-ty-RAN-us)

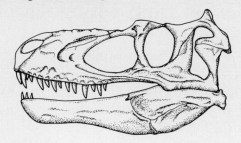

▶ Whether it was a juvenile or an adult, *Nanotyrannus* clearly ate meat. Just look at those daggerlike teeth!

✳ **NAME:** *Nanotyrannus* means dwarf tyrant
nanus (dwarf) + tyrannus (tyrant)

○ **FAMILY:**

Saurischian
Theropod
Tyrannosaur

✛ **SIZE:** perhaps 16 ft (5 m) long; perhaps 4 ft (1.2 m) high at the hip

⚖ **WEIGHT:** about 880 lbs (400 kg)—about the same as a polar bear

FOOD: meat

HABITAT: forests

N **WHERE:** remains found in Montana

🕐 **WHEN:** 69–65 million years ago in the Cretaceous period

NANOTYRANNUS

TRIASSIC	JURASSIC	CRETACEOUS	
250 MILLION YEARS AGO	205 MILLION YEARS AGO	135 MILLION YEARS AGO	65 MILLION YEARS AGO

Nemegtosaurus

Nemegtosaurus was a sauropod, a big long-necked, long-tailed plant-eating dinosaur. It is known only from a single skull, collected from Mongolia's Gobi Desert in 1965.

The shape of its skull tells us that *Nemegtosaurus* was a sauropod. However, because fossil-hunters have not found any other *Nemegtosaurus* skeletons, it is hard to decide which type of sauropod it was.

How did it live?

All other sauropods ate plants, so it is likely that *Nemegtosaurus* did too. Its teeth are long and

BRINGING IT ALL BACK HOME

Paleontologists have explored the Gobi Desert for over 70 years and have found the remains of a number of sauropods. In addition to *Nemegtosaurus*, two other sauropods have been found in this area—*Quaesitosaurus* and *Opisthocoelicaudia*. Like *Nemegtosaurus*, *Quaesitosaurus* is known only from a single skull. For *Opisthocoelicaudia*, paleontologists have the skeleton of the body but not the skull. Although several sauropod specimens have been discovered in the Gobi, only a few have been transported to museums. The fossils are large and are found in wild places.

Hunting for dinosaurs in the Gobi is tough work. Fossil-hunting expeditions have to take everything they need with them. There are no stores or gas stations. There are few roads and terrible dust storms. Water is scarce. Yet the Gobi is still paradise for paleontologists because of the many fossils buried there.

▶ **Nemegtosaurus** is known only from its skull. However, paleontologists can reconstruct **Nemegtosaurus** using what they know of other sauropods.

DINOFACTS

Nemegtosaurus
(nem-EGG-toe-SORE-us)

 NAME: *Nemegtosaurus* means lizard from Nemegt
Nemegt (region of Mongolia) + sauros (lizard)

FAMILY:

Saurischian
Sauropodomorph
Sauropod

 **SIZE:** unknown but perhaps 50–70 ft (15.2–21.3 m) long;
8–10 ft (2.4–3 m) high at the hip

WEIGHT: unknown

FOOD: plants

HABITAT: broad floodplains next to large rivers

WHERE: remains found in Mongolia

WHEN: 69–67 million years ago in the Cretaceous period

			NEMEGTOSAURUS
TRIASSIC	JURASSIC	CRETACEOUS	
250 MILLION YEARS AGO	205 MILLION YEARS AGO	135 MILLION YEARS AGO	65 MILLION YEARS AGO

thin and would not have been very useful for chewing. The edges of its teeth are worn away. This suggests that, like *Diplodocus*, *Nemegtosaurus* used its teeth to nip leaves and shoots from tree branches.

Because *Nemegtosaurus* was a sauropod, it would have had a long neck which it could have used to reach up into tall trees to search for food. In the Late Cretaceous period, the area where *Nemegtosaurus* lived had plenty of surface water. There were lots of plants, so finding food would not have been too much of a problem.

The last sauropods?
Sauropod fossils are rarely found in rocks from the latest part of the Cretaceous period, just before most of the dinosaurs died out. Most of the sauropods that have been found from this time come from South America.

Nemegtosaurus was one of the handful of sauropods that lived in other parts of the world in the Late Cretaceous period. It is not known why sauropods were so rare then, as they were extremely common during the Jurassic period. Perhaps the plant-eating sauropods could not eat the new plants that evolved during the Cretaceous period. It is hard to say for sure, though, because paleontologists have found so few of the fossils of all the animals that ever lived.

CHECK THESE OUT!
Cretaceous period, Digging dinosaurs, *Diplodocus*, Extinction, Jurassic period, *Opisthocoelicaudia*, Plants, Saurischian dinosaurs, Sauropods

Nodosaurus

Nodosaurus was an armored dinosaur that roamed North America in the Early Cretaceous period. Unlike some armored dinosaurs it had no club on its tail. Its tanklike armor was a good defense, though.

Paleontologist and dinosaur collector Othniel Marsh described *Nodosaurus* in 1889. One of Marsh's collectors found *Nodosaurus* during an expedition to Wyoming. The collector was returning to camp one night when he spotted some dinosaur remains.

The specimen was not complete. It included bits of the forearm, hind legs, the upper part of the hips, part of the tail and back, and some armored bumps. Marsh

recognized that these pieces of bony armor formed rows of small bumps and larger, flat-lying plates across the dinosaur's back. Scientists still do not know whether *Nodosaurus* had bony spines sticking out of its side, as some other nodosaurids, such as *Edmontonia*, did.

▼ Collectors have found only parts of *Nodosaurus*'s body; they have never found its skull. Scientists and artists reconstruct the dinosaur by looking at other nodosaurids, such as *Sauropelta*.

Clubtails and bare tails

Nodosaurus was the first ankylosaur (armored dinosaur) ever discovered. There are two groups of ankylosaurs. Ankylosaurids, named in honor of *Ankylosaurus*, have tails that end in clubs. Nodosaurids, named in honor of *Nodosaurus*, have no tail clubs.

Lumpers and splitters

Scientists disagree about how *Nodosaurus* is related to other nodosaurids. New England paleontologist Walter Coombs has lumped it together with other nodosaurids, including *Sauropelta*. He believes all these nodosaurids are the same dinosaur. Other researchers such as Denver Museum's Ken Carpenter think only Marsh's 1889 specimen is *Nodosaurus*. They believe the others are different kinds of nodosaurids. Scientists need to find good nodosaurid skeletons to help them solve this puzzle.

How did *Nodosaurus* live?

Nodosaurus probably ate low-growing plants. It probably escaped meat-eating dinosaurs by hiding from them. If found, its armor could withstand an attack by small meat-eaters and perhaps even by larger dinosaurs.

CHECK THESE OUT!

Ankylosaurs, *Ankylosaurus*, Collecting dinosaurs, Cretaceous period, Ichthyosaurs, *Sauropelta*, Thyreophorans

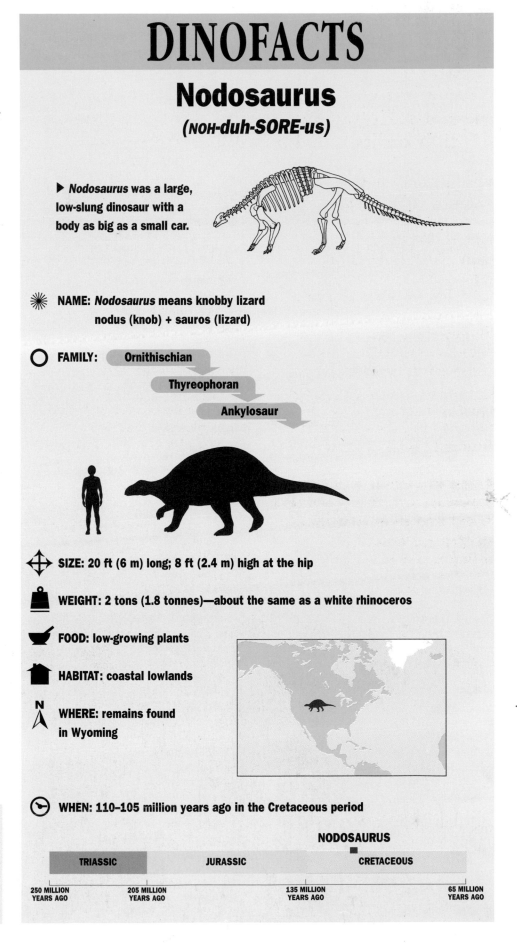

DINOFACTS

Nodosaurus
(NOH-duh-SORE-us)

▶ *Nodosaurus* was a large, low-slung dinosaur with a body as big as a small car.

✳ **NAME:** *Nodosaurus* means knobby lizard
nodus (knob) + sauros (lizard)

○ **FAMILY:** Ornithischian → Thyreophoran → Ankylosaur

✛ **SIZE:** 20 ft (6 m) long; 8 ft (2.4 m) high at the hip

⚖ **WEIGHT:** 2 tons (1.8 tonnes)—about the same as a white rhinoceros

⚗ **FOOD:** low-growing plants

⌂ **HABITAT:** coastal lowlands

N **WHERE:** remains found in Wyoming

🕐 **WHEN:** 110–105 million years ago in the Cretaceous period

			NODOSAURUS	
TRIASSIC		JURASSIC		CRETACEOUS
250 MILLION YEARS AGO	205 MILLION YEARS AGO		135 MILLION YEARS AGO	65 MILLION YEARS AGO

Index

Page numbers in **bold** refer to main articles.